Notes of
a Reluctant
Pilgrim

Notes of a Reluctant Pilgrim

The Idea of Pilgrimage in Everyday Life

CHERYL FORBES

ZondervanPublishingHouse
Grand Rapids, Michigan

A Division of HarperCollins*Publishers*

Notes of a Reluctant Pilgrim
Copyright © 1992 by Cheryl Forbes

Requests for information should be addressed to:
Zondervan Publishing House
Grand Rapids, Michigan 49530

Library of Congress Cataloging-in-Publication Data

Forbes, Cheryl
    Notes of a reluctant pilgrim : the idea of pilgrimage in everyday
life / Cheryl Forbes.
      p. cm.
    ISBN 0-310-75551-4 (pbk.)
    1. Christian life—1960- 2. Christian pilgrims and pilgrimages.
I. Title.
BV4501.2.F5895   1992
248.4'63—dc20   91–36403
                                                    CIP

Printed in the United States of America

92 93 94 95 96 97 98 / ML / 5 4 3 2 1

To John Alford and Marcie Williams
Guides Unaware

And to Bob Hudson
a True Signpost
for the Wandering Writer

Contents

I cannot keep my subject still. It goes along befuddled and staggering, with a natural drunkenness. I take it in this condition, just as it is at the moment I give my attention to it.
—Montaigne

In Preparation

....

Numerous pictures over the centuries have helped people understand what life means, for within all of us is the instinct, the longing to go beyond the physical to reach a sense of the spiritual significance of existence.

The apostle Paul was fond of the metaphor of the race. He also used the idea of a journey, a trip, a pilgrimage, to explain what life is all about. St. Augustine too favored the idea of life as journey. But it was Jesus who used it before either Paul or Augustine when he said, "I am the Way"—the footpath, the track, the straight and narrow, which we reach through a squeezer or stile. As Augustine believed, Jesus is both the footpath to the destination and the destination itself. Perhaps this is why, despite religious differences, despite cultural and technological differences, so many readers and so many writers have for so many years found in the metaphor of pilgrimage a metaphor that gives shape and meaning to life. This book, itself a pilgrimage, explores what it means to be a pilgrim today.

Since I first envisioned what you hold in your hands, several years before I began writing, I have traveled a long way—back through my childhood and into my future. I have also traveled centuries into the past to look for the spiritual and psychological paths that have created me and my culture, which itself has traveled some pretty tough terrain lately, and no one quite knows how the trip will turn out or who will guide us. My journey has surprised me at every turn; it has frequently frightened me by its painful insistence that I tell the truth. It has forced me to see all the personas I present to my world, including the persona I am in this vision. It has also assured me that not all personas are lies.

Notes of
a Reluctant
Pilgrim

Starting Out

....

All the old tales, to use a favorite phrase of C. S. Lewis, tell
us that pilgrimage begins in the spring, in May or April,
when the sun is soft, and the breezes too. It's not soft
outside my window, if I had a window to look through
where I write. But I know there is neither sun nor breeze
this morning—a wind, yes, and a wind chill, two degrees
above zero at 5:30 a.m. when I first encountered the
outdoors on my daily dogged jog.

No person who intends to be a pilgrim would begin
on such a day of snow and ice and wind and weather.
This is a day to read and rest, a fire comfortably burning;
this is not a day to walk and work and wander through
the weather. But this is the day I have, and pilgrims, or
would-be ones, can't wait for the right moment. Is there
ever such a time?

I begin this book during the first week of Advent
1989. Advent. An appropriate time. A solemn time. A
time to begin a pilgrimage, at least the kind of pilgrimage
we will go on. But to begin now violates all the ancient
traditions, though even its violation makes Advent appropriate, for Advent startles and disturbs us, because it is
both secular and sacred, perhaps the only holiday we
have that falls into both camps, which puts us at sixes and

sevenses. Advent does what pilgrimage does, whatever the season—raises questions, puts us off balance, disturbs our security.

What are we during this time of year? Consumers? Or are we waiting to be consumed by the awesome God who comes as an infant needing care? That's one too many paradoxes for a would-be pilgrim. And yet, isn't the startling and disturbing aspect of being a pilgrim the fact that it *is* paradoxical, a sacred and a secular event, an act that violates chronology because no one does it anymore? It doesn't fit with our society, whose idea of pilgrimage is a ski trip or two weeks in the Holy Land.

Looking back, which writers and pilgrims need to do a lot, I see I called Advent "solemn." Another paradox, another misfit. The last quality of Christmas is solemnity. Jingle bells and bobtails. Blinking red and green lights. Blaring, bouncing commercials pleading for business. What is solemn about all that? Frenetic, yes. Dazzling, almost blinding, yes. Certainly excessive. I have never, not once, seen bed and board less than sumptuous at Christmas. I am probably more guilty of this than most, my kitchen thick with the incense of butter-rich cookies. Eat, drink, and be merry, words wrenched out of context, sum up the season. Where's the solemnity or, even more farfetched, the sacrifice? Somehow, at least in some of the old books on pilgrimage, that word wriggles in.

But this juxtaposition of opposites—solemnity and sumptuousness, sacrifice and celebration, the opposites that slam at us as at no other time of the year, underscoring that pilgrims live neither totally in sacrifice nor totally in celebration but in a movement between the two—not only makes pilgrimage appropriate now but necessary, *if only* to work off some of the cookies we've consumed.

Perhaps we sacrifice out of guilt for our Christmas indulgences, but so be it: If it leads to the right road, why quibble?

Yet the ancient tradition and symbol of the Christian life isn't popular any more, even among Christians, the fault, perhaps, of the gasoline engine: We don't walk enough, we don't get dusty and bone-weary enough. What walking we do, especially during Advent, occurs under the mall roof, great insulation from the elements.

So pilgrimage and sacrifice are out of date. In my mind the two are connected, because it takes a lot of sacrifice to become a pilgrim, especially with the baggage we carry. Maybe society has it right and the Church wrong. Christmas is coming, not the crucifixion; let's celebrate, not suffer. Let's leave that for the few who note the forty uncomfortable days before Easter. We in the Church have Lent and Easter all to ourselves. Few stores beg us to buy their Easter bargains. It's hard to get sentimental about a bloody cross; a baby is another matter.

Yet no matter how appealing it might be to put on brocade and black tie, forgetting all that solemn stuff, I cannot conclude that the Church is wrong to be the only voice for suffering and sacrifice now, in part just because of the contradictions inherent in the season, for they become a metaphor for all that Advent is or points to and all that pilgrimage means. Advent, as the Church calendar determined, would focus our attention on preparation for the coming Lord—and in ancient terms to prepare means to sacrifice and to repent.

Repentance is such a loud word that it, as perhaps no other word is able, drowns out the jingle bells and smothers the Christmas clothes with sacks of ashes. No one can become a pilgrim unless he first rejects the values around him, repents for having embraced those values, and throws off the green and red garments for ones very nearly resembling the clothes of John the Baptist. Because pilgrims travel light, the dress that society would have us don simply weighs too much for the journey.

John knew that, just as he knew where any pilgrim needed to begin. He was not the first pilgrim to find his way to the starting place—we need to go all the way back to Abram for that, maybe even to Eve and Adam—but for those of us living under the New Covenant, John seems the best model for what it means to be a pilgrim today, even when most of us won't wear sandals and sway through sand to the Jordan River.

At least not literally. We have no choice but to go there in some way, and metaphor may be our only road. It's hard to envision what a pilgrimage is like today or what being a pilgrim means, simply because we don't set off one day, leaving our lives behind to walk our way to the Kingdom. Maybe Mother Theresa can, maybe St. Francis could, but we can't. Even if we didn't have so much responsibility, what with the car payments and the mortgage and saving for the kids' college, we aren't trained for such travel.

But Advent tells us that we've got to go, *if*, that is, we want a look at the leader, which is why every Advent the first hymn we sing takes us to John.

> *On Jordan's banks the Baptist's cry*
> *Announces that the Lord is nigh.*
> *Awake and harken, for he brings*
> *salvation from the king of kings.*

John knew we'd be doing some traveling and even speaks in those terms when he explains to *his* followers that he is unworthy to tie the sandals of Jesus. The minimal preparation for any journey is getting the footgear laced correctly, yet John can't do even that for Jesus.

If only that were all the Baptist gives us—but it isn't. John speaks with a harsh and grating voice, telling us the road to the Messiah is tough traveling, despite his making the rough places plain and the crooked straight. No one told John that this isn't the way to write a travel brochure, not today. As a publicist he rates pretty low by giving about as dismal a picture as he possibly can. Where's the four-color photography? The high-flying slogans? You know, something like, *Pilgrimage. It's more than a place. It's a state of mind.* Something that appeals to our psychology or our love of adventure-without-commitment. The ultimate in wilderness training. Progress monitored by your wrist computer at the push of a button.

Such talk, however, isn't for John. The rough places and the crooked roads—our sins—that's the pitch he uses. But we've grown comfortable with them, like a broken leg that has healed crooked. We don't want it rebroken, no matter how much better it will be when it reheals. This, though, is the only offer John makes at the beginning of Advent, the only metaphor he's got. If you want to see the Lord, get ready for rough terrain.

So the Lord comes, first as an infant, then as a child, and finally as the adult we know as Jesus. John has issued a call of pilgrimage, a call of repentance, a call to get on our feet, but not a call to follow him; that's where Jesus takes over and the real pilgrimage begins. The other was mere preliminary—making our reservations, getting our tickets, packing for the trip. A one-way trip, for once we've begun there's no turning back. Abram knew it, as do pilgrims today.

Follow me. Those are the words of Jesus; all else is mere commentary. Many of us say, Why not? Might be fun. Things have gotten a little dull anyway. Life is too easy. Time for a challenge. Time for a little physical exercise—not too much now, but a bit of muscle-stretching might not be bad. Now where did I put my camera? I've got to bring back pictures, otherwise the folks'll never believe the places I've seen. Oh, look at this luggage. I can't take this stuff with me, looks like some rat's been at it. Well, I've always wanted a matching set. And clothes. These clothes will never do. Can't take chances with the weather. Could be cold, could be hot, could rain, could snow. And provisions. Yes, a few Hershey bars are in order, because who knows whether the road has any vending machines. Be prepared.

This sounds nothing at all like a pilgrimage, where we can't be prepared and don't have space for suitcases of any kind. Rather, it sounds like the talk of tourists, who buy a round-trip ticket, a way out—for they intend to return. Tourism isn't permanent; it's merely an interlude to the daily routine. Tourists want to see the sights all visitors are supposed to see, but only long enough to take a few pictures, buy a few postcards. Their interest doesn't run off the well-traveled track to dirt paths or overgrown lanes where a pilgrim might find herself. The agenda is packed too tight for more than a quick look at the must-sees; tourists don't plan to live long, if at all, out of a suitcase, not to mention a backpack.

The pilgrim road may provide momentary interest as a break from the normal routine, but it's hardly a comfortable way of life. And it's a good bet pilgrims get blisters, even with the right gear, at least until their feet harden to the journey. Tourists don't come back with calluses the way John the Baptist does. As pilgrims setting off in winter, we should expect chilblains and frostbite before we reach our destination.

Suddenly, this doesn't sound like such a good idea; I may have talked myself out of a winter pilgrimage. The old tales are right—warm weather, that's the stuff for pilgrims. People are too busy during Advent anyway—I know I am—to take off right now. I mean, don't I have a book to write? Becoming a pilgrim is too serious a decision to make in haste, only to repent with frozen knuckles.

Anyway, you may not be reading this during Advent, and snowflakes may be a distant memory. Maybe you've just picked your first ripe tomato and buttered your first sweet ear of corn. Perhaps you're resting in the hammock after a bout with the lawn mower or the charcoal grill. Nothing like barbecued chicken, right? Chilblains and calluses are the farthest things from your mind. A tall glass of ice tea is more like what you need, or a good rain to cool things down. All this talk of winter walking sounds too forbidding—not that a walk in such heat appeals to you either. But that's pilgrimage.

A pilgrim, as I said, has no choice but to walk whatever the weather and to begin regardless of the circumstances. If it's hot where you are, then heat is the perfect weather for pilgrimage. I'm sure I can make a case for it, if I try. Let's see. John the Baptist spent a lot of time in the desert; that's one reason. And there's always something to be said for the purifying prescription of sweat and labor. That's two. And what about this? It might take even more effort for us to move in the summer heat than in the winter cold.

This is starting to sound hard again. No, summer is far from the ideal time for pilgrimage, I can see that now. Besides, if we leave, who will pick the beans, not to mention the zucchini?

Maybe we ought to put off this pilgrimage until fall, after the last of the tomatoes have been canned and the sun has moved a little farther down the line so it isn't beating directly overhead. Well, I don't know. Is fall any better? Things pick up in the fall, like school and concerts and Halloween. Then there's Thanksgiving; to miss out on the turkey and stuffing would be downright un-American. But if we don't go during fall we're right back to Advent, and we already know how hard it is to do anything then, even if it is appropriate. So are the old tales right? Is it spring or nothing for a pilgrimage?

The air smells sweet during spring, when we can smell, that is, what with mold and grass and trees to aggravate the allergies; nothing is worse than a runny nose on a pilgrimage. Spring can be unpredictable too, hot one minute, cold the next. The backpack can get pretty heavy, having to accommodate such a changeable season. It usually rains a lot during spring. I can already feel the cold trickle of rain snaking its way down my neck and see the stream of water falling in front of my eyes as it runs off the bill of my hood. I know my hands are a rough red, not numb enough to block the cold, just cold enough to make them stiff. What happened to the sweet showers and soft breezes Geoffrey Chaucer promised at the beginning of *The Canterbury Tales:*

> When April showers have killed the March droughts and every plant has drunk deep, soon to show its flowers; when light, sweet breezes inspire every hill and heath—then folk long to go on

pilgrimages, to seek the one who has so often cured
their ills . . .

This sounds like the medieval version of good marketing
strategy, like postcards of Great Britain in which the sun
always shines when we know that's hokum. I'll bet old
Geoff never walked from London to Canterbury in April;
it makes a good story though.

Here is where a tourist has an advantage over a
pilgrim. What difference does the weather make to a
tourist? His matched luggage carries everything he needs
and covers every eventuality. If he did overlook a small
detail, or if the travel agent forgot to remind him to plan
for something, he can always head for the nearest castle or
the local pub for a pint and a platter of fish-and-chips to
wait until the nasty climate turns nice again. If the
accommodations lack amenities, move on, for there's
plenty of petrol in the tank. If the trip turns really bleak, a
slap of plastic on the counter and a tourist takes the next
flight out.

But a pilgrim? A pilgrim writes a different story. At
the end of a rough walk a pilgrim will take any shelter he
can find, even a rock out of the wind. He's got no other
transportation than his feet, and he can't play the plastic
game when he's walking on a one-way road with no place
to turn around.

This is getting worse and worse. Being a tourist
sounds much more attractive than being a pilgrim, which
may be why there are so many tourists and so few
pilgrims; the tree-lined avenue is always more appealing
than the footpath through the nettle patch. It sounds as if
I'm talking us out of pilgrimage. No season really works,
no time is really right, no road lacks potholes and pitfalls.

What does that make me—a reluctant pilgrim? Probably. I suspect we'll find lots of us on the road, just as I suspect that lots of people will wonder, if pilgrimage is so uncomfortable, why bother? A fair question, a central question for us comfort-loving creatures, though not an easy one to answer. (Remember, we're the ones who invented the shopping mall.) Why *do* we put ourselves in the way of hardship?

Without violating the principle John the Baptist established, truth unadorned with fancy marketing gimmicks, we need to remember that along with the hardships John mentioned come strength, satisfaction, glory, life, in all their long and honorable history. Although these abstractions appear in all kinds of dress, those are the abstractions we're seeking that we can find nowhere except in pilgrimage: Tourism doesn't do it. The longing for them overcomes our reluctance and our fear that we might not be up to the journey. We probably aren't. But who is? Which is another paradox of pilgrimage, as well as another comfort, because being ready is irrelevant, just as waiting for the right time is irrelevant.

So if I'm going to go, I've got to go now, and as I said, it's cold and it's snowy and it's Advent. I leave with the holy family, all of us starting a journey that is uncertain at best. I may be fleeing for my life as the holy family did, or I may be walking to register myself as belonging to Bethlehem: It might take a few miles to find out.

You may come along or simply imagine what I'm going through, just as I can imagine what you're going through during the spring rains or the summer swelter. Or we can admit that you and I and all of us who have given pilgrimage a good long think and have decided, despite its drawbacks, that we really have no choice but to become pilgrims, will sooner or later be walking when it's cold, hot, wet, or dry. If we aren't prepared to walk regardless of what may come, then we'd better not walk at all.

A pilgrimage can begin at any time, in any place, and take us through all seasons and to more places than we would ever have thought possible. Sooner or later, though, all true pilgrims arrive at the same destination, having met the same sorts of adventures. How something can be so individual and so universal at the same time is a mystery. Although I may never travel the same road you do, yet when we compare maps and journals how is it that they look so much the same? How is it that I can understand your experience as a metaphor for my own? And you can understand mine?

This business of being a pilgrim certainly can be a grab bag or maybe a white-elephant sale where we never know what it is we've bought, what the value might be, or why something we learn to treasure became another person's junk. What made *us* buy it when someone else gave it away? Why did we make the commitment with our one-way ticket when our neighbor said, "No way—make mine round-trip?"

We travel together as we travel separately—and that's also part of the pilgrimage puzzle. Our paths cross the paths of tourists. Same roads, but different destinations. And so many questions, more questions than answers. How is it possible to travel the same road and end up at a different place or to travel different roads and end up at the same place? How can I go west and you go east and we both get north? What happened to those people who were traveling west with me? Did they retrace their steps or take a lefthand turn while I was studying the map or looking for the gnarled beech the directions mentioned?

There's almost no predicting what can happen on a pilgrimage or who your fellow pilgrims will be—another grab bag. We have no assurances that we'll even like or trust each other, any more than Chaucer's Miller and Reeve, or Paul and Luke, liked and trusted each other. Well, even arguments can be beneficial by keeping our minds off our aching feet. Certainly the disciples in their wanderings kept up a patter of debate that seems exhaustingly relentless to us today who are used to reception not interchange; for all our talk of communication, we're a pretty silent bunch by comparison to the people in the old tales.

The old tales. I see that I've used that phrase three times now and probably will again. We share with every modern generation a disdain and a disrespect for anything ancient; at best we insist on reinterpreting it to make it relevant. Can someone who knew nothing more high-tech than a camel—or her feet—talk to people who mention moon trips as casually as they talk of trekking to the movies? But the old tales, or an old tale retold, may be better fare than any new tale we might read, because we need wisdom, we need understanding, we need to know what it means to be a pilgrim and how to keep walking when the terrain toughens under our feet and our feet refuse to toughen to the terrain.

A stroll through wildflowers with springy turf beneath and blue sky above is one thing, and we'll surely have those times, but what becomes of us in barren landscapes of rocks and cloudy gray, we who aren't forced to foot it too often? Then we need the advice of someone whose feet are the natural and necessary mode of travel, not one who travels by foot because it is a luxury to do so, which lets out all of us today, myself included, because I don't have to walk anywhere or for any great distance except by choice (or because my car won't start in this frigid, Advent air). Although we would welcome a shot of sun, we need more than that.

Walking and pilgrimage—those two ideas, those two metaphors, those two realities—cannot be separated. When I walk, I connect myself to all those pilgrims who have traveled the ancient paths before me, crossed the same stiles, squeaked through the same squeezers, crushed the same corn, and all for much the same reason—to get from one place to another without fumes or fossil fuels, to root myself to the earth, to understand its contours, to contemplate the destination, which cannot be separated from the road itself.

When I walk I think of my physical surroundings—it's hard not to—but I also think of my spiritual surroundings, perhaps in part because the physical and the spiritual are inseparable. Perhaps we know the spiritual through the physical, and walking is one metaphor that comes alive for us most when we do it the way those in the old tales did it, with a minimum of protection and a staff to help us up the steep slopes we will all encounter.

When we walk we become part of Chaucer's pilgrim crew contemplating Canterbury (to see the tomb of the "holy blissful martyr," Thomas à Becket) and telling tales to pass the time; we become Christian in John Bunyan's *Pilgrim's Progress*, suffering through the Slough of Despond or fending off Vanity Fair; we become pilgrims to Lourdes, Jerusalem, Bethlehem Ephrata; we become the pilgrim disciples traveling with our Lord toward Golgotha without knowing the trials to come. We become all these and more—pilgrims pounding our way along blacktop and tar, through malls and materialism, past televisions and computer technology, to find that narrow path where cars can't go. We learn what it meant to be a pilgrim, as we learn what it means—different tenses, different surroundings, but the same destination. We learn whether we can even read the old tales with more than surprise and curiosity; we learn whether the old tales can become our wool and leather.

So walk with me. I'll tell you a tale of pilgrimage, beginning with what may seem *in media res*, in the middle and not at the start, though, as I've said, pilgrims take off from anywhere at any time, and sometimes we're halfway down the road before we realize we weren't ready to set off, before we remember, like poor huffing and puffing Bilbo Baggins in Tolkien's *The Hobbit*, that we forgot our handkerchief and that we don't like adventures.

But marked for adventurers we are; so off we go, hoping that there's more about us than meets the eye, our eye, at least, and that the wind won't blow too bitterly out of the north as we face the final days before Christmas.

Lost

....

John Wayne leans down over his horse, hands gripping pommel and reins, stares at us strangers, and says, graveltoned, "Where're ya headed, pilgrim?" Or so my husband recalls, and when he thinks of pilgrims, John Wayne, not Chaucer, hoves into view.

We don't know much about being pilgrims today; we don't even think of the word, much less the entire context that the word points to, its long history and culture, or as Lewis Thomas would say, "its conversations with itself"; even words become pilgrims, as the word *pilgrim* has done. It has traveled from its literal meaning in the early church era, through the Middle Ages where it had its heyday, and down to John Wayne. At least he asked the right question, even if a pilgrim is a little bamboozled as to how to answer it.

To answer the Duke's question honestly, most of us itinerant types might reply, "How do I know? I'm a stranger in these parts. I *thought* this was the way to the Celestial City or the Emerald City, but somewhere I made a wrong turn because I've been wandering in this desert so long I've forgotten what green looks like."

The Duke draws in a deep breath and drawls out, "It sounds to me like you just might be lost."

Lost? Mistaken, maybe, or misdirected. "But," we shout, as we wave something in the air, "look at our directions. We couldn't be lost." Then we consider the desert, horizon to horizon, and wonder if the Duke isn't right.

Putting spurs to his horse, John Wayne gallops into the sunset. The daylight is dying, the temperature dropping. Time to reconnoiter, preferably under the protective heat of a boulder. We spot one just up ahead, not too far. Adjusting our packs, after pulling on sweatshirts, we start forward, forgetting how deceptive distances are in such territory. Eventually, we reach the rock, but not before another sweatshirt comes out of the pack, this one with a hood. Flopping down, we take a new look at the directions, which still make no sense, and think again about the Duke's question: "Where're ya headed, pilgrim?"

Actually, until we heard the word, we hadn't understood we *were* pilgrims. Accountants, bankers, lawyers, teachers, mothers, wives, siblings, husbands, steel workers, students—those are the words we define ourselves with, not pilgrims. We have to admit, though, the word seems to cover just about everything that's been happening. We woke up one morning, pulled on our new shearling slippers, and found that our feet hit hot sand and not hardwood and braided rug. How, we don't know, but suddenly we were in the midst of a Franz Kafka parable, just thankful to be still human and not beetle. Our job was gone, our security shot, our sense of direction as befuddled as a compass whose magnet can't find north.

If the Duke had only asked where we were headed a few months ago, we would have had some answers. Up the ladder, out to the country club, into a Porsche, on a plane for the Columbia River, Tiffany's for breakfast—all the best places people like us can head for. Then we turned in our tourist badge—or had it taken from us, we've never been certain—and found sand and dirt and enemies wherever we turned. All of it a lot more than we bargained for.

"Where're ya headed, pilgrim?" Where do we *want* to head? Isn't that a better and easier question? Each of us, once our adolescent confusion dies down, has a pretty good idea where we want to head. For lack of anything better we can use the word *goals*. That is, there are things we want to do and own. We want to travel to London or Paris or James Herriot country; we're interested in tourism.

So far as goals are concerned, some of us want a good job and a nice house; others want a sailboat or a cottage on prime trout water. Lots of us want a family with two smart, good-looking children, a boy and a girl. And most of us want enough money to live comfortably, whatever that means, which is a problem, of course, because comfort used to mean a pot of soup on the stove, a loaf of bread on the table, and a good fire to warm us. Now it takes more than soup and bread and fire to comfort us, and it takes a lot more money. Although a pot of savory lentil soup can still be had for under a dollar, now we need veal medallions and candlelight, wall-to-wall carpeting and cashmere sweaters—which puts us considerably above a dollar for just the veal alone.

But what do we need with cold-weather comforts when we've been traveling through the desert, though night has fallen, and a cashmere sweater—no, make that a down jacket—would be in order? These sweatshirts, no matter how we huddle together, aren't keeping the cold at bay. Our companionship isn't keeping the fear at bay either, the terror of not knowing where we are.

It's that word *pilgrim* that does it. How can we answer, "The corner office in corporate headquarters," when John Wayne wonders "Where're ya headed, *pilgrim*?" The corner office is too trivial a destination next to that ancient, weighty word. And if corporate headquarters is no longer the destination, then what is? Can pilgrims wear pinstripe suits and power ties? Maybe, but they aren't the clothes best suited for movement.

If nothing else, *pilgrim* implies a journey. The four walls of a corporate office, no matter how spacious, don't take much walking to circumnavigate, though it might take considerable navigating to get there. What once looked like a good goal becomes upon arrival a cage that isn't large enough to contain our restlessness. Not even the local mall can do that, no matter how much money we throw at our economy—and we do try to help it all we can, thinking, none too altruistically, that really we are helping ourselves reach the destination we determined for ourselves when we took our first job out of school. It is activity of a kind, but movement without purpose, like an arrow without a point.

So here we sit, huddled against a boulder, which is getting colder by the minute, trying to sort things out, trying to decide whether we should follow the Duke and turn back or whether for all its drawbacks the desert is better than the boardroom. As with most things in life, inertia cradles us; the known is better than the unknown, the here-and-now better than the what's-up-ahead or behind. Only when inertia decides it has had enough and chucks us out on our ear do things start to churn, which always seems to happen at a strategic point in the pilgrimage. For now, however, inertia is content to let us rest, helping us argue that anyway it's too dark to turn around.

So we return to the original question, which leads to several more. Where *are* we headed? What's the point? What is worth giving our life to or for? Not what we thought. That much is clear. We shake our heads with the irony—just like most things in life, right? Looks can be deceiving. You can't tell a book by its cover (tell that one to the publishers!). There's more to this than meets the eye. Can we think of any more truisms that cover the situation? Shakespeare's Polonius (from *Hamlet*) would be in his element right about now: "To thine own self be true"—what a lot of bunk that advice is and probably has caused half of the world's miseries, first in trying to figure out what *self* means and then in trying to figure out what *true* means, and finally in trying to figure out how to put those two together. If Shakespeare had only known that the words he put in Polonius's mouth would end up as "do your own thing" or "you've got to take care of your own needs first," he would have pitched his pen. Just like us to misunderstand that he was mocking Polonius, not seriously suggesting the old bird's philosophy as worthy of adoption. That nonsense is a pilgrimage right to the center of our navel, which is even tighter quarters than the boardroom. But there's no doubting that Polonius would have had a ready answer for this situation. No stumbling and inarticulate grunts for him.

Somehow, though, the ready cliché doesn't answer for our situation, huddled together against the night and wondering with Tolkien's irrepressible Bilbo Baggins why we ever left on this adventure but knowing full well that some change is occurring within us that we don't want to stop. Oh, it isn't only that we've trimmed a few inches from the middle, which we'd been trying unsuccessfully to do for some time. No, it's something else, something that doesn't meet the eye but that we sense is growing from a seed into a sproutling. Not something Polonius would notice, since he does judge a book by its cover and won't even buy one that doesn't promise platitudes on every page and easy advice for mall walkers and materialists: He wouldn't like this one.

There now. I've given away the secret and so soon— I'm not going to give any advice, for I have none to give. All I can narrate are the stories of pilgrimage and how all the stories have one thing in common: Change. We change because the questions change. We can't predict what they'll be, so there's no predicting where they'll take us. Questions are like contradictory road signs: Which ones do we follow? Maybe part of being a pilgrim means learning which questions to ignore.

But the question that puzzles me now is this: How, given the glorious destination our directions indicate, can we be traveling on such a miserable, hard road to get there? I mean, if we wanted to visit Buckingham Palace we wouldn't take a rat-infested, garbage-reeking, back alley, now would we? But here we are, huddled against the cold, with a lumpy pack for a pillow, supposedly on our way to royalty. None of this makes much sense.

If this were a Zane Grey novel things would probably take a nasty turn; we've got all the elements we need. It's cold, dark, uncomfortable. It might even start to snow. Our supplies are running low; there's no fresh water to replenish our canteens. A wolf howls, and we wait in dread for the sound of a rattler. All these things, metaphorically speaking at least, could cause a lot of trouble at this early stage in our pilgrim journey. But they don't.

It's enough right now to be cold and tired after a day's walk. It's enough to long to take off our heavy boots, though we know we can't in case our feet swell. Probably the best thing is to sleep, if only the packs weren't so lumpy. But "sleep knits up the raveled sleeve of care," speaking of Shakespeare, as we were a moment ago. And things look better in the morning, because it's always darkest before the dawn. So let the great sleeve-knitter begin, and wait for sunup. Surely something will occur to resolve our pickle and get us out of our dilemma.

Despite the worries I fall asleep immediately, just as the books say pilgrims do. But the books don't talk about the dreams that come, unless we count William Langland's fourteenth-century poem *Piers Plowman*, one strange medieval dream after another. There's something to be said for having a guide explain things as a dream progresses, kind of a live-in therapist. Today, though, we wouldn't find the character of Holy Church, one of Langland's guides, helping out, since that's the last place most of us go when we need some explanations. No, we would find Therapy or Self-Actualization a more congenial consort; even that shows a shift in attitude, since dream-guides were charged with correcting evil, not promoting congeniality.

She—for some reason guides are often female—would reassure us that this is only a dream but that we might have much to learn from being unable to flee from a monster who bears such a strange resemblance to the colleague we've been cutting for the past week. Or Therapy might ask us to think about why we get satisfaction from such behavior, as we dream about the time we were eight and the neighborhood bully shoved a bag over our head and grabbed our hard-earned Good Humor bar. But always Therapy would ask us to find our own answers, not point to Right and Wrong. Although we want to answer our own questions, we also would like someone to say, "Here it is. The Right Answer. Do this and all will be well."

Will, the hero of *Piers Plowman*, isn't the only one to have a guided tour of dreamland. We can't forget the indefatigable Scrooge, especially at Advent. His three guides took him on a quick life journey that turned his values on end.

Yet my dream has been nothing like Scrooge's pre-Christmas adventure, nor like the dreams Will had. No Holy Church to guide me—just me, a wanderer without clothing, without protection of any kind. My dream had no beginning or end; what dreams do? I merely drifted into the dream, or should I say that I suddenly knew that something was going on. I was watching myself wander, but I couldn't understand why. I seemed to be searching for something. Clothes, first of all, because I looked cold. After I spotted a familiar sweater, I put it on, though I inconvenienced someone to retrieve it, which was true for all the other belongings I located. Jewelry was especially hard, because most of it was scattered throughout a cafeteria, which had scratchy seat cushions that snagged my necklaces and earrings. As if that wasn't bad enough, I had to interrupt the meals of many customers to reach what belonged to me. I stretched my fingers to pick up a slim gold chain and thought I had a firm grip on it only to have to try again and again as the customer became more and more irritated. Who could blame him?

I was too confused to be irritated that someone had scattered my things everywhere. Why would someone do that to me? How did I let it happen? I didn't know I had so much jewelry, but the task of collecting it took longer than my meager belongings should have required. But in dreams we don't stop to consider what we're doing or why, we just react, as I did, continuing to wander from place to place in an effort to pick up every piece of cheap jewelry I ever owned.

Here's where an astute interpreter would have been handy. She might have noted that this jewelry stood for all the parts of my life that were in disarray, or for the parts I thought important but that seemed silly and inconsequential to other people, an inconvenience. Perhaps the dream was merely a midnight replica of the pilgrimage we've begun, a pilgrimage that didn't look to have any rhyme or reason, any goal, but as I collected my worthless jewelry it began to shape itself. Had John Wayne appeared in this dream and asked, "Where're ya headed, pilgrim?" I could have said, "Wherever I need to go to pick up all these pieces." Which may not be a bad definition of pilgrimage, at least to begin with.

But because I had no guide to make the most of the dream, I was in and out of it before I could shift positions on the unforgiving sand. Flat on my back now I stare at the stars, noting that the sky is different in the desert than in the city. Pilgrimage seems so un-American, so contrary to John Wayne himself, the quintessential rugged individualist who rides alone to conquer evil. But here we are, not alone, not rugged, yet definitely committed to completing a journey of uncertain expectations and guarantees, not that we hadn't received some promises.

Daylight. I don't understand how you slept so

soundly, but the snoring said you did. You seem to be winding down, right on cue. There, the first orange-pink streak in the sky and you swallow your final snore and sit up. The sun lights up the boulder, giving the illusion of warmth, which should cheer us considerably, but you appear to have gotten up on the wrong side of the sand. I'm cold, thirsty, and hungry, not to mention this side of crazy for a cup of Colombian, strong and hot. I've never been much of a breakfast eater, as you know, but I do like my daily cup of coffee. If you start in, this is going to be one long day, not to mention pilgrimage. No wonder Bunyan had his hero travel by himself, a violation of pilgrimage but much more serene. No, I'm not snappish—you are. Why are you blaming me? You're as responsible as I am for our predicament, maybe more so. You insisted on making that turn back there. Oh you did, did you? Wanted to turn back? So why didn't you, then?

It was a good thing you held up your hand to show me what was happening. When we were warned of enemies we never thought of dissension, bickering, accusations—and we have fallen prey to them all without a thought. It probably won't be the first time, as anyone who's lived with other people knows; at best we're cactus characters. Just look at those folks poor Moses had to handle. Not a please or a thank you in the lot. Now that I think about it we face the same enemies they did, but again without the comfort of a *visible* guide, just as in my dream: fear, confusion, uncertainty, exhaustion, lack of vision, all of which sound very much like the spiritual condition of modern society. I expect to hear someone shout, "What's the point of living?"

I prefer the words *Where are you headed, pilgrim? What are you doing? Why are you doing it? Where do you think it'll land you? Is it worth the effort? What will you gain if you do reach your destination?* We want answers to these questions, and we want them with such desperation that we will go to almost any lengths to find them—or if the final despair sets in and we decide there *are* no answers, then we will do anything to pretend the questions don't exist or that they are mere philosophical murmurings of an untidy mind. Yet they are the questions that started us on this pilgrimage to begin with, so we can't avoid them.

I read a letter in Ann Landers' column right before we left. The desperation of the first sentence gave the prose great power, which kept me reading. It was the story of a woman's struggle to survive the pilgrimage she had begun (though I have no idea whether she was traveling to the same destination). Married with two children, this woman had to work to make ends meet, not, as she said, to live luxuriously; the couple's income together was modest. She was tortured by what she saw as the neglect of her children, the result of having to work, though if she quit she would hardly be able to feed and clothe them. So she was forced to choose between which kind of neglect she heaped on them. But not only was her time with her children limited, so was her time with her husband. Not that she faced housework and child care without his help, but nevertheless she still found herself working late and getting up early. Stretched to the breaking point, this woman was also fighting a severe weight problem. Carrying almost 100 pounds too much would tax anyone's energy. But like so many women she ate to compensate for the frustration and anger she felt. Trapped. *Trapped,* I could hear her say. And she knew it was a life sentence. I have never read anything so hopeless or wondered with such certainty how long before this woman decided to cut short her life sentence.

It seemed to me then as it seems to me now that she epitomizes the pilgrimage too many of us are on. We don't know how we got started and have no idea when it will end, but we know we're going nowhere except in circles. We're cats chasing our tail, thinking at first that our tail is the goal—only to pause for breath and realize what we've been doing. For some of us, as for this desperate woman, we don't know how to do anything but chase our elusive tail, so we keep at it, year after year, circling slower and slower with the passing time and increasing arthritis. Even a cat eventually decides this tail-chasing has had its day, but we don't seem to have such wisdom.

Now, however, you and I are on a different kind of pilgrimage.

Walking in Circles

....

Yes, we're on a different kind of pilgrimage. Or are we?

We need to consider this question before we go much farther, for if the Duke's question was shoeleather tough, this one is like eating a Goodyear tire for breakfast. *Are* we any different than the woman so desperate that Ann Landers is her only hope? I answered yes with such certainty because we are pilgrims.

But perhaps it is presumptuous to assume that pilgrimage immunizes us from our culture. I wonder whether her experience isn't the necessary and unavoidable nature of human existence, even regardless of culture. Night. Day. Sleep. Waking. Work. Rest. Hit the alarm, roll out of bed, shower, dress, fix and eat breakfast, get the kids ready for school, pack lunches, do the dishes, rush to work. Then back home at the same time each night to fix supper, eat, do the dishes, read to the kids, go to bed. And the next morning we hit the alarm, roll out of bed. . . . Around and around in circles, day in day out. I suppose that Homer and Chaucer also experienced such debilitating repetition, though the mark of our culture may be that we experience them as burdens driving us to distraction and despair, rather than shifting our shoulders to bear their weight with muscles accustomed to the work.

So comes the problem: How to make something as circular as living into a pilgrimage, which implies something linear, something from here to there, something with a destination. Or to put it another way, How can we know meaning in such an existence?

When I think of that question my old Slinky toy comes to mind. In searching for a metaphor to explain how "circular" can go somewhere, I begin to recognize why the Slinky fascinated me as a child—circles that moved forward or, the way I used it, from up to down. I went up the stairs and followed my Slinky down the stairs. Once it started to move the destination was inevitable, though its movement wouldn't have been so inexorable had it not been for its circularity.

If we have enough circles and something or someone to propel those circles forward, we end up going somewhere. My husband tells me that this is a mathematical principle, which I'm glad I didn't know when I was playing with my Slinky: Math and I weren't friends. If I drew my Slinky toy, its behavior that is, I'd be drawing a *hypocycloid*. In the two-dimensional world of pen and paper we'd see it move forward, creating loops on a plane, intersections that disappear almost as soon as they form, rather like the road a pilgrim travels, where he joins others for a time, only to loose them to intersect with others—or the same people?—further down the path.

Think of a Slinky toy. As the toy moves forward, the circles, or loops, that it forms disappear even as it is in the process of forming new loops. Every new loop puts the toy further along even though it keeps repeating the same activity, over and over and over. A constant movement forward despite the round and round of returning events. But looking at this figure in three dimensions, something different happens: The circles become a spiral, which I think of as rather like a twisty, hollow line, something that no longer touches the road (or the imaginary plane of our two-dimensional existence), but becomes the road itself, because I can climb it. I can get inside it and use the circles to propel myself on my way, something I couldn't do with my Slinky. With it, I was only the observer.

Looking back on my childhood from this circle-destination perspective, I recall lots of circles that went somewhere, circles that I moved or that moved me, where I was participant and not simply observer. Penmanship class, for instance. We were taught the Palmer Method and learned to make big circles and little circles from the lefthand side of the page to the righthand side—a destination—with the final destination good handwriting, or a completed sentence, a line that *says* something, even if only big and little letters or "the cat jumped over the hat." But that physical exercise was intended to lead to an intellectual abstraction, the notion that there existed something called educated penmanship, that the form in which we constructed the meaning was as important as the meaning itself, or to use Marshall McLuhan's well-known phrase, "The medium is the message." My teacher, however, was not at all interested in the larger philosophical questions that the Palmer Method raised; perhaps she would have been better off teaching us calligraphy.

But I had many other circles in my life—snowballs, for instance. I recall one in particular that I, my sister, and a group of friends rolled up our hill; it collected more and more snow on its way. So what started as a modest little snowball truly did snowball into something that none of us could wrap our arms around. The only thing to do with such a giant snowball was shove it on its way back down the hill, where it might have formed the base of an impressive snowman, another collection of circles, though immovable.

An eight-year-old doesn't mind running in circles, whether it's rolling tire rims, keeping a Hula-Hoop going around and around her waist, or trying for the double-dutch jump-rope record. We even went round and round the pond where we skated without a twinge of regret, and we had no greater fun than to make ourselves sick and dizzy by spinning round and round while looking into a hand mirror at the ceiling (try it sometime). If anything, circles were at the heart of our best inventions, not a cause for despair.

But hypocycloids, Hula-Hoops, and the Palmer Method, Slinky toys, and snowballing snowballs only take us so far as metaphors for pilgrimage, because pilgrimage implies not just movement from one place to another but that movement has meaning as well. Which takes us back to the beginning in true circular fashion, for meaning implies movement, which implies change and growth. It implies that you and I won't be the same for having experienced meaning, however it comes, whether through the Duke asking us an embarrassing and pointed question like, "Where're ya headed, pilgrim?" or someone else asking, "Do you have any idea why you're walking through this desert? What's the point of it all?"

Peggy Lee asked such a question in a hit song some years ago—as unlikely an inquisitor as we might find, but one appropriate for our culture. "Is that all there is?" she crooned—and we wondered with her, Peggy Lee suddenly the popular existential philosopher. To some of us, her question sounded like the modern refrain of the ancient author of Ecclesiastes who complained about vanity and bemoaned that life held little meaning. People live and die, the sun rises and sets—and we're back to our circles. It seems that we cannot escape the connections between our life and those who lived long before Johann Gutenberg invented the printing press or Alan Turing conceived of the computer, when writers used papyrus and quill, not microchips and RAM (Random Access Memory). Vanity is the ancient metaphor for life's meaninglessness just as pilgrimage is the ancient metaphor for life's meaning; and the two are intertwined then as now.

So whether Peggy Lee or the Preacher of Ecclesiastes uses the language that captures our culture and our imagination, they both lead us to the same road, where we set out to discover if that's all there is or if anything other than vanity exists under the sun. Only those fundamental questions can cause us to shoulder our pack, lace up our boots, and head out. The problem so many of us desperate people have is that we find ourselves moving a lot without finding any purpose in it. Not that this is all bad, for sometimes the only way to discover purpose is to get going, not worrying at first how clearly we can sum up in three neat points where we've been, where we are, and where we're headed.

Another paradox every pilgrim faces: We've got to know why we're walking at the same time that we recognize we haven't a clue. An odd thing about pilgrimage is that some of us begin the trip convinced that we understand it, only to discover that the longer we travel the less sure we are about what we're doing. Along the way, our purpose has lost significance for us—that in the circles we run we fail to find or recognize anything worthy of so much expended energy, because traveling in circles is no less exhausting than hauling ourselves through the desert. I find myself back with my Slinky toy, which, for all its charm and movement, did nothing more than entertain me for the few harmless hours I spent going up and down the stairs, conveniently out of my mother's hair; such activity delights a child—but an adult playing at Slinky toys is a much grimmer picture.

So how can we have begun a pilgrimage through sand and snow, rock and ridge, when we still face these endless circles of dishes, trash day, laundry, and credit-card bills? I nearly envy those people who took pilgrimage literally, something us Westerners no longer do. (I have to add a caveat, because millions of people in the world still do make literal pilgrimages each year, and some of them are from the West, but wouldn't we characterize them as superstitious, clinging as they do to some simple-minded notion that the physical and the spiritual intersect in such an act?)

I wish I could do what people no wealthier than most of us did—take several months, a year, or three, to walk a pilgrimage. Something important happened when a group of pilgrims bound themselves together to wander their way to a holy shrine. It was no small commitment, and the enormous effort called for no small sacrifice.

What would happen to me if I could do that? What would happen to the people who traveled with me or to the people I met along my journey? Is a lifelong commitment to a metaphor, to seeing life as a pilgrimage, more meaningful than a year spent going on one? If we tried it—just for comparison—what destination would we find holy enough to warrant uprooting ourselves for any length of time, intending to return only when we have satisfied ourselves that we have walked into what life means? Is there an answer to be found? Most of us would rather have the answer show up at our door than for us to step out to find it.

That conjures up some interesting images—a path presenting itself to our feet instead of the other way around, as if a ceiling suddenly turned into a wall or a floor, as it does for Mary Poppins. Things can be topsy-turvy, whether Tuesday or not, so that we might find ourselves having tea on the ceiling; a path, though, that walks to us rather than us *on* it? Maybe we're suffering from an overdose of sugar and air conditioning, a deadly combination, two standard ingredients in our way of life that we don't share with the past (we forget that sugar once was as scarce as salt).

Yet materialism—and sugar and salt—has a great deal to be said for it. We're more comfortably housed, clothed, and fed than anyone ever has been. We don't lack toys and gadgets to titillate our fancy or to push life into convenience. Given a certain amount of money, we even can be insulated from certain necessities of life (as the aristocracy once was), from shopping, cooking, cleaning, childcare; the difference, of course, is that what once was the province of the few is now available to more and more of us. With the time that gives us, we have created lots of shrines—Disney World or the Hall of Fame—another interesting contrast. Pilgrims, or the merchants who catered to pilgrims, if such people existed (maybe inn-keepers are the closest we can come) didn't create shrines; shrines came into being because people believed that something significant and *life-changing* had happened there and could again. There was nothing artificial or manufactured about holy places, though there might have been fakery and deception.

We, on the other hand, have no end of artificial shrines. Yet we lack a sense of the sacred, though some of us might say that a visit to Cooperstown or Graceland is by way of a visit to Canterbury, that the Babe's bat or an Elvis guitar is a relic worth contemplating as much as the tomb of Becket. Pagans, of course, have it all wrong when they fall at the foot of a tree or at the paws of a cat, but at least they don't lack a sense of awe or an understanding that there are large forces about that need not consider paltry human beings. Well, oldstyle pagans, anyway. Modern pagans fall at their own feet, a pretty trick that resembles nothing so much as stumbling.

We might say that oldstyle pilgrims too have it all wrong. What good does a walk to Canterbury do? Or a climb up Loughrigg Fell, that shrine of nature lovers? Are we any holier as a result? Or any wiser? Are we any closer to the real destination than if we'd stuck it out at home, relishing our roof, our heat, our burgers and fries? I'm not sure we can answer those questions without giving the literal a try, at least occasionally, so that we learn to move between the literal and the metaphorical with the same ease that we walk down the aisles of a grocery store.

Even those not used to walking. The Northumbrian coast of Great Britain, next to Scotland, can prove formidable for those who know the terrain and are outfitted properly. But for a sedentary Shakespeare professor and his wife it can be downright daunting. Only a longing to look at Lancaster Castle—which plays a silent but central role in so many of Shakespeare's history plays—could make such folks succumb to the need to be on one's feet.

"How far to the castle?"

"Just up the way" (undoubtedly an American translation). I can hear the thick, broad accent of those who live
north of the Umber River, so difficult for even other
English people to understand. Perhaps the couple misun-
derstood the directions, for they determined that such a
short way was manageable, even in such weather.

I didn't mention that, did I?—that the weather was
intent on drowning anyone who ventured forth. Soon the
couple was drenched to the skin, hardly a surprise in the
English climate. Rather, in retelling the story, the man
revealed the shock of most Americans who follow an
English footpath for the first time: The path leads anywhere, and sheep and cows and humans yield to it. In the
circular fashion appropriate to this chapter, as he retold
his story he returned again and again to the footpath—to
the cows, to the pastures, to the rain and mist, to the
castle they never seemed to reach. The elusiveness of their
quest encouraged them to keep walking, though every
few minutes they asked each other, "Should we turn
back?" "I think we should turn back." But they couldn't,
after having come so far, just give up.

And what they would have forsaken if they had.
Finally, through the palpable darkness—a Monet painting
in reverse, all shadows and dreams, not light ashimmer—
they caught the outline of the castle. And it caught them
by surprise, as if such a sight were impossible. With every
footstep closer it took on the solidity that the word *castle*
conjures up, until they stood at its door. And it stood
angle and edge on the cliff that blocked the sea from its
foyer. The sea that day was a turbulence to be reckoned
with.

As the professor groped for words to convey an
experience that was obviously beyond the power of his

language to reveal, he finally settled on pilgrimage. "I remember thinking at the time that my wife and I were pilgrims of a sort, though whether I consciously used that word I don't recall. But the force of our walk was that—it made us pilgrims."

All sorts of experiences can become pilgrimages, even to those who had never thought in such terms. Having seen Lancaster Castle as it was meant to be seen, the couple will never read Shakespeare's *Richard II* as they did before. In admitting himself into the company of pilgrims, at least for this experience if not for life, he spoke as if changed. "I'll never forget that sight," he concluded. It would be too much for me to say that his voice indicated longing for return; I'll leave that for lovers of nineteenth-century poetry. His very matter-of-factness told the tale, as if giving me the dimensions of the impression Lancaster Castle had embedded in him.

It was my discussion of this book that prompted his memory, convincing me again that everyone has within them a pilgrim story, a pilgrim desire. Situations like this have happened often, as if no one can hear enough about the pilgrim way—and often those who seem the least likely to become pilgrims are those most interested. This metaphor has power, perhaps the reason so many writers, Bunyan and others, have used it. It makes sense of what we're about, or ought to be about. It makes connections between the spiritual and the physical. It makes believers of us, even though we still have plenty of questions.

But first we walk; there will be plenty of time for questions later. If we start with the questions, as Jesus understood, we'll never shoulder the pack and stretch our legs for the long haul. We can become too interested in commentary for our own good.

So for at least a day this Shakespeare professor and his wife forsook their material comfort, a necessary prelude to the pilgrimage. Their material comfort, however, made their pilgrimage to Lancaster Castle possible, just as our material comforts do, even though we have to turn our back on them if we want the kind of experience pilgrimage provides, or even if we only want to jump off the Ferris-wheel routines we find so distasteful. Perhaps we even tolerate the circles so that we can once a year, or once every other year, dispense with the routine to go from here to there and back again, like a child moving from class to recess and back. We know we can't have both simultaneously.

Tourism is the closest we come to the ancient pilgrimages. Does it matter that the destinations are the castles of Europe or the gardens of Great Britain rather than the Sea of Galilee? There are worse places to visit than Lancaster Castle. We have choices that no literal pilgrim ever dreamed of—horseback riding tours, garden tours, restaurant tours, great-writers tours, even cathedral tours, which could at least cause someone to stumble onto the path of a true pilgrimage. For every interest and budget someone somewhere will offer a tour.

Reading the four-color brochures and full-page ads always makes me ready to sign up, because the copywriters and photographers and design people always know what appeals to me, the lush gardens or the rugged castles that reveal their age and dignity. I'm as gullible as anyone and as resistant to the anti-marketing of true pilgrimage. I long to know what it must have been like to live in Lancaster Castle. But my longing is only vicarious. Or remodeled, just like the castles. Put me back there only so long as someone has installed central heating and indoor plumbing; for the rest, I'll resort to imagination or the odd book. Any closer than that and my nose starts to run and my shoulders to shake from the cold.

In other words, I'll willingly take pilgrimage on my own terms, but not on the terms pilgrimage may offer. And so copywriters promise me that by way of the tour I will know the life of a lord of the manor. Better and better. Which fits in perfectly with my personal image, since I never see my Self as serf but as Lord (never mind that I would have been male, not female). If they give me the biggest room, I might even be willing to put up with a simple in-room heater rather than central heating.

Perhaps more than anything else, a tour promises a larger-than-life experience, *meta*life, to use the current jargon—Fantasy Island where all our dreams become metadream. We can hardly claim reality, since part of the pull is that we know none of the trip is real; nor do we want it to be. We're paying for a dream and mean to have a doozy. Plain, old, ordinary life, the kind we started this chapter with, is what we're escaping from, the drudgery that is the necessary and inevitable consequence of existence. Not even a four-star tour can remove all the consequences, of course; we will fight colds, headaches, stiff muscles, irritability, and all the rest, despite lying where King Richard did when he was struggling against the ague or Henry IV struggling with penance for his sins. We will quibble about whether to have a cream tea or an early supper, whether to visit a museum or walk another footpath tomorrow. Haven't we already had a fight or two? The compensation, I suppose, is that we won't have to mow the lawn, take out the trash, or shuttle the kids from baseball practice to piano lessons. We've reneged on those responsibilities, for a while, at least.

Which tour have you picked, supposing we can get ourselves out of this desert and back to a major metropolitan airport with nonstop connections to anywhere in the world—Singapore or London, Paris or Abudabi? Airports have us running in circles; and airplanes keep us circling the airport, flying nowhere. We don't much like airports, but is there a more appropriate oasis for our time? No matter where we look we find places we must travel through to get through to the travel. And airports have their compensations today, if only croissants and Dannon yogurt. Our desert is making me long for a glass of juice, and I don't see any palm trees or orange groves up ahead. Maybe an old-styled oasis is as out of fashion as this stuff about being a pilgrim. Right about now the sight of a jumbo jet has great appeal. I imagine that we'll see more of airports than sand before we're done.

But back to the question. I'm leaning toward a tour of the Great Castles of Britain, though the one on gardens also appeals to me. Maybe the Great Castles also have Great Gardens, a winning combination. What do you say? Shall we stick together? At least then we'll know one other person. Not that I mind traveling with a group of strangers, which might be preferable to traveling with friends or family, a far greater commitment. We can always ignore the strangers if we find them stranger than we'd like. Well, maybe not ignore them, but at least not talk too much. If we don't talk to people we know well, they'll hound us to know why—got up on the wrong side of the mattress? Cat got your tongue? Did we offend you somehow? Boy, are you crabby! Strangers would just dismiss us as curmudgeons or snobs. Of course, that attitude violates the community intent of pilgrimage, but so does a tour.

The advantages of a tour, just as with our materialism, need further consideration. More than just the
promises appeal to me. For a few weeks you and I, who
spend our life taking care of others, will experience the
luxury of being taken care of. It is all carefully planned,
even to the places the bus stops for people to buy
postcards. Insulation, that's what tourism touts. Insulation from the elements, from discomfort, from the society
the tour travels once over lightly. Even walking is held to
a minimum, which, considering the shoes most of us wear
when we walk our tourist path, is a good thing. But above
all that tourism promises to provide the dream of aristocracy, of wealth, of class and privilege, which brings us
back to Lancaster Castle. But dare I mention such notions
in a culture that claims to be founded on classlessness?

I must admit how attractive tourism sounds. We
never doubt where we're going, how long we'll be gone,
what we'll face while we're gadding about; tourism is as
predictable as life can get—secure and safe, especially
with a tour guide as guard. Well, why not? It wasn't so far
back that I, caught in the desert with only you and a
boulder for comfort, was bemoaning our lack of a guide. If
only I had remembered that a guide is easy to get, we
might not have found ourselves watching the dust of the
Duke's heels with our spirits sinking more rapidly than
the sun. Surely, with tours of all kinds we could find one
that was headed our way.

And what if we do? It's there and back again. It's
traveling round and round. Tours become merely another
kind of circle that we travel feverishly, hoping for some
entertainment, some break from the mundane circles we
run when we aren't touring. But is there really any
difference? A tour maintains a schedule—up at a certain

time every day, breakfast at the same hour, and probably the same breakfast if the travel occurs in Great Britain, stopping after so many hours for a bathroom break and a quick trip to buy postcards, back on the bus, and . . . Circles. Bigger circles, maybe. More expensive circles, certainly. But circles. They trap us into having fun, and we dare not admit that fun is not what we find. The travel brochures, once more, have promised more than they deliver.

We can't say the same about pilgrimage. It promises us a lifetime of walking and a bog or two midway through the journey; even the best-planned pilgrimage, if that is not a contradiction in terms, gets mired at times. Pilgrimage delivers on the hardships, just as it delivers on the rewards and satisfaction of striving together for meaningful existence.

We pilgrims lose our way, no matter how well-marked the path, sometimes because we choose to leave the path, despite the warnings never to do so. Or we forget that we are pilgrims, not tourists, and hook up for a time with a tour group, trading destination for circularity. Breaking out of those circles is hard, especially when we remember how lonely the search for the way back can be. It is also difficult to look foolish around people we want to impress; leaving a four-star hotel for a hostel, or worse yet, no hostel at all, strikes those in a four-poster bed as a foolish way to spend a night, not to mention a lifetime.

Even if we don't think about impressing people, we still don't want to look foolish—inept, odd, ridiculous, out of step. Pilgrims are the two left feet of society, the people who wear different colored socks. What is the old phrase? *A peculiar people.* It takes a lot of fortitude to be an oddity, to move left when everyone else is moving right.

We may even appear peculiar to those we thought were fellow pilgrims who, with the excuse of understanding the other side, move right with everyone else. What a shakeup that causes within us, but beneficial, for it forces us to check the path and the waymarks to make sure we've been reading the signs correctly.

Reading the Signs

Reading. How can we miss the way if all we need to do is read? Because we had no problem reading the travel brochures, even the fine print, I know nothing's wrong with our eyesight. And it's not as if we even have to read *words*; colors will do—yellow, red, or blue—arrows will do. We're following a color, just like Dorothy in *The Wizard of Oz*. But if I remember, didn't she get lost too, following a yellow brick road? How much more obvious could the path have been? Yet we're walking a dirt path— foot, cow, or sheep—overgrown with nettles and thistle; occasionally we find an arrow splashed with color.

You don't see one yet? We will find our way eventually, despite this strange detour through the desert. I admit we haven't chosen the most direct path, but when pilgrims set out sometimes the important parts of the journey are those that edge the path or go off it. Never mind that we find ourselves in the desert, because we realize, now, that we might not read as well as we thought we did. Something miscued us, some ambiguity of language that led us accidentally to the wilderness.

But can there be accidents on pilgrimage? If we're walking into the old tales, then the wilderness is the first step in that direction, because that's where the pilgrims in all the oldest stories find themselves first: a prerequisite to the rest.

I read (present tense). Somehow that word keeps cropping up—ubiquitous, inescapable. I read the dictionary. I read the wilderness. I read you and me and our relationship. I read what I have written, what you will read. I read to discover if what I have written and then read—past tense—will help us learn that the wilderness becomes the place to begin the journey, to start the questions, to learn which signs to read and heed and which to ignore. The word *read* recurs as often as the old tales themselves, and I suppose that's as it should be. What we read, whether the old tales, this tale, or the new tales of travel brochures and slippery slogans, will send us in one direction or another and will determine what we will make of the journey once we've begun.

The wilderness, for instance, can either make or break us. It *ought* to strengthen us for the hazards ahead. That reluctant pilgrim Bilbo Baggins didn't deal with the dragon until long after he had some serious walking under his belt, which was better than the extra flesh he'd been carrying at the outset of his adventure. The Israelites couldn't appreciate the milk and honey until they'd thirsted for forty years. Even Jesus had his days in the desert. Perhaps we've made too many assumptions about pilgrimage, or too few, or even worse, the wrong ones. Misreading—isn't that what landed us in this sand to begin with? I remember a prime case of misreading that cost miles and many minutes, a situation not unlike the Shakespearean scholar and his wife, except that we had better weather.

Allen, my mathematician husband, and I had been doing some careful reading, or so we thought, stopping every few feet to check the directions, to check the map, to check the compass as we walked through the Cotswolds region of England. When pilgrims plan to travel through three villages in a day, it's wise to avoid misreadings, especially at the start of what will be a long walk. With every stop we assured ourselves that we indeed were reading correctly; we greeted every waymark as further confirmation that this time we wouldn't lose our path.

The sun stretched high by mid-morning, and we lengthened our stride on the hard-packed path, evidence of the drought in Great Britain that summer. Although we worried with the farmers, we reveled in light packs and gear. As we hummed along, we greeted fellow travelers heading in the opposite direction—a mother and son, a collection of men and women, who were members of a walking club, the odd cow and occasional horse. The contours of the Cotswold hills rolled beneath our feet, the white clouds rolled above, providing just enough shade to belie the fact that we were in danger of sunburn. After pausing to grease our arms, legs, and faces, we continued our way to the ruins of a medieval church and monastery—tenth century, as my recollection and my journal remind me.

Christianity had come to Great Britain two hundred years before then with Augustine the missionary (not the St. Augustine who served as bishop of Hippo in the fourth and whose *Confessions* have served as pilgrim guide ever since). How long it had taken Christianity to move from the south of England, where Augustine preached, to this part of the country, sort of west midlands, I did not know, but I suspected that we were on our way to one of the earliest churches in the area. A shrine, we could say. A holy place. A testimony to the power of the faithful, though how much the people maintained their ancient rituals, such as well dressings and maypoles, I wondered.

But two hundred years from the beginning of Christianity on the British Isles to the ruined rubble we anticipated was a blink of the eye. We were eager to see the remaining structures and to compare them with other ancient testaments to Christianity that we had visited. Would we read, as we had in a previous visit to another part of Britain, the roll of faithful ecclesiastics, even to forty generations or more? Such connectedness to the earliest touch of Christ on the shoulders of unlettered people whose only reading could come in the form of the original Word was a longing not to be delayed or denied.

As I've thought about this problem of reading, I've wondered who is more fortunate, those of us on the other side of Gutenberg, or those without benefit of book. Looking at the Word from that perspective changes the perspective. The notion of Scripture is not one, then, so much of something printed that I can hold in my hands and reread whenever I choose. Rather, the Bible is always something spoken, something mediated by the person who can read the words to the person who can't, to me as a member of that community who attends this church as it first stood, whole and useful and necessary.

I don't understand the option of print; the idea of daily devotions as *reading* is wordless, bereft of language and therefore sense. The early church wouldn't have understood such an emphasis on text, either. When Christianity confronted pagan classical literacy, the spoken word, not the elitist notions of literacy, won. The gospel traveled by foot and by spoken word first; only later did writing come into it, and even then the written was heard. No one sat in a corner, isolated from community, and read to herself.

If this option of print is meaningless, then some other ritual must stand in its place—matins, mass, messages in stained glass—some other means of literacy. I am hearing and remembering; rising and standing; bowing, kneeling, reaching, lighting, moving within the context of the message to physically enact something metaphysical, something spiritual, yet made concrete in the living language of the sacrifice and my obedient response to it. For the unlettered, it cannot be something abstract or something spatially less than multidimensional, unlike the rest of us who experience the Word as flat page, flat type. Because I cannot hold stained glass or the cross, I know that this greatness come to earth is beyond me at the same time that it is part of me, part of my condition, part of my community.

On *this* side of Gutenberg, however, we can hold the Incarnation in our hand, shrunk to the confines of nine-by-twelve in black or burgundy leather, a faith we can understand, a person we can control. Or so we infer from the object, whether or not the inference is correct or conscious. We can insist on fidelity to this print in a way that not many would have understood when Augustine touched Great Britain. Which is truer, I wonder? The Word spoken, the Word revealed in flesh and blood, the immediate intercessors between us and God, or the Word read to myself without community? Which is easier to misread?

Probably both are susceptible. If only reading were as easy as misreading. In my admittedly romanticized portrait of this anticipated church—its bare but not barren sanctuary, with the rising and falling congregants living on the rhythms of the spoken Word—I find great appeal, though my knowledge of how incomplete their understanding of the faith they adopted makes me temper my desire to return to prebookish days. The very event of my writing rejects such a notion, as it asserts the importance of print, the importance of book, the importance of Western, literate acts. Nevertheless, my love of reading, made possible by the printing press, as well as our corporate reverence of the Bible, cannot make us forget that there are many ways to read and many ways for God to make us pilgrims. It doesn't depend on a page of print, no matter how important we believe that print to be.

And yet how would I know something of the church we are walking to meet without that technology? My ability to imagine an unlettered community of believers only comes, paradoxically, because of the lettered community of which I am a part. The words lead me to become a member of the kneeling, rising, bowing, worshiping community I referred to earlier, the clouds of faithful witnesses I read about in the New Testament. I read the words, I incorporate the words into my consciousness and memory, I live and relive the words as I pilgrim through the Cotswold hills on my way to the rubble that once was a place where the mysteries of the faith were enacted.

But as I said, all words are susceptible of misreading, and this day is no exception. Once we became caught up in the journey we forgot to check our directions with the compass. We'd been right so far. As soon as we find ourselves thinking like that and behaving without regard to our unerring ability to err, we go wrong.

Allen and I reached the gate at the end of the field just as our map said we should. Now which way? With no waymark signs in sight, we decided to head right up the lane, which seemed to be the direction the directions indicated, though the compass didn't agree. Do we go with the compass or with the words? Being people on this side of Gutenberg, we chose the words. We walked and we walked and we walked. Beautiful honey-colored cottages line the lane—and some hideously anachronistic cottages as well. But, though we enjoy the lane, we didn't seem to be any nearer our destination. *Isn't the church supposed to be to our left?* we ask each other. *How will we get there?* We saw no signs, found no breaks in the hedgerows or fences. When the lane climbed sharply up toward what appeared a dead end and the start of a farmer's field, we knew we'd once more misread the directions, how we didn't know. That's the frustrating part about misreading, figuring out what went wrong when we thought we were attending to every word.

By now the sun was heading toward its high-sky mark; breakfast was hours past, and we didn't want to stop for our field lunch until we'd reached the church and gone beyond it. *Can we wait that long to eat? We can wait, provided we find our church soon.*

For some reason, as we've all discovered, returning seems to take less time than going, perhaps because the way is now familiar, so we soon were back at the gate. Shrugging out of our packs, we rechecked directions, compass, and evidence of some waymark. All we knew was that the right hand is not the right turn. A long time to learn a simple lesson. With no other options, we decided to head straight across the next field, hoping that it was a legal footpath or that if it wasn't, our status as inept Americans would protect us, always our line of last defense.

Only later, on our way back to our lodgings, did we

discover what we had done wrong. But at the time we only knew that, somehow, we finally had rejoined the right path; a waymark sign on the final fence provided assurance. By then, though, the church stood in our sight, so there was no mistaking. When we reached it, framed by smooth-worn gravestones and high grasses, the church was not the rubble my imagination had reduced it to. It was lovely, yet lonely, despite the visitors. Relics of all kinds seemed to suffer loss. This church had been made for living worship, not for a curio of a time when such things meant all things. So while a few tourists took pictures outside—and we eventually did the same—we entered the church, not the first we had visited; nor would it be the last.

It was the kind of church we wanted to find. Although we had visited some of the great cathedrals of England—like Canterbury, Salisbury, St. Paul's, Westminster Abbey—and had seen some of Europe's finest— like Cologne and Munich, we now looked for the small, isolated parish church, the kind with room for thirty to fifty parishioners, who once huddled together against the cold and the devil. A person can feel displaced in the soaring space above her, though intellectually I accept the meaning of the space and believe that there are times when a cathedral preaches just the sermon I need. But for this day, at least, I needed to hear what this small Cotswold church might say.

We always take our time inside such a church, even though time is one of the dimensions without great meaning there. That too belongs more to a cathedral, just as space does; perhaps that is why I prefer small churches to large. Because there isn't a great deal to look at, there's more to be part of, more to contemplate. A small church insists that I join the history of worshipers, whose acts still linger in the air. And again it reminds me of those clouds of faithful witnesses. They tell me to sit or kneel; they compel me to open the worn book of prayer, to fit my hands to their hands in the work of worship, to find the thumbprints impressed over the years.

Work and rest—simultaneous, oxymoronic. And I remember the easy yoke, the light burden, and wonder at how deeply embedded such contradictions are in the faith I profess. Even the walk of the pilgrim is a contradiction, as this book is, because we have been talking of pilgrim and pilgrimage as a way we go, something we move toward, as Christian in *Pilgrim's Progress* moves ever closer to the Celestial City. And that's both right and wrong, both an appropriate metaphor for what happens to us on earth, and an inappropriate, because incomplete, metaphor. As literature professor Stanley Fish put it, in a Christian plot, taking plot as metaphor for the story each of us writes as we live: "If [Bunyan's] Christian is to be truly in the way, the way must first be in him, and then he will be in it, no matter where—in what merely physical way—he is." To be on the path means to have within ourselves the path, which is another way of saying what Augustine said: Jesus is the way to the destination and the destination itself. Jesus put it even more succinctly, "I am the way."

So we both follow the path toward our destination at the same time that we have the path already in us. No wonder we can lose our way so easily—like following the tip of our nose. And this path, this plot, is, again in Fish's words, "haphazard, random, heedless of visible cause and effect, episodic, inconclusive, consisting of events that are both reversible and interchangeable." That about sums it up, this life we lead, this pilgrimage we travel.

It is comforting, however, that where we are may not ultimately matter, so that all lost paths become a new path, all misreadings of the signs become a new, potentially right reading. And eventually, somehow, we find ourselves on the way to the church. But we don't like to do it wrong, even if we get it right in the end, and Allen and I, at least, tried to discover where we missed our mark. On that particular day, we learned upon our return what had happened. How? We looked up.

Such a simple event and one we should have thought of when we found ourselves misdirected. Experienced pilgrims know that a sign can occur anywhere, on a street curb, on a fence, on a stone wall, on a tree, or, in this case, high overhead on the only available space—a utility pole. There it was, faded with the weather, but still unmistakably a red arrow. At the time the incongruity didn't strike me, though now as I consider it I see how incongruous it was. A utility pole stands for modern life—everything that pilgrim life stands in opposition to, or at least at angles with. I can accept a waymark on a two-hundred-year-old tree or stone fence, but a sign on a sign is one too many layers for me. Aren't I trying to escape such signs by traveling to a church that never knew electric lights and artificial heat? Why, then, should I expect the way to the church to be painted on a pole?

But there it was, merely another paradox of pilgrimage and a reminder that Jesus said we were in the world but not of it. And to be in this world of ours means finding the way out of this world through things like utility poles, computer-generated texts, and television screens, as well as the ancient signs of trees and stones. I can't even recall what directed our attention up to a sign that by its very context seemed to deprive it of its purpose, rather like giving someone a drink of water in a sieve. Not much thirst-quenching will go on.

No, perhaps I shouldn't have used that image, with us still in the desert, though it does make the point. Being surrounded by sand focuses the mind in certain grooves. At least we have each other to talk to. I've often wondered how Jesus survived with no one around until Satan showed up. Such isolation devastates the human psyche. We can bear almost any other privation so long as we can talk about it, but to be hungry and thirsty and *silent*— except for our own voice—seems beyond the power of any of us to withstand. The silence must have been the worst of Jesus' trials, so that he was ready to listen to anyone, no matter what the person said. Recognizing this makes his resistance so much more remarkable.

How many of us would have been able to resist the conversation of Satan regardless of what it was about? Just to hear another voice and to find ours a little rusty from disuse would have made us susceptible to sin. Perhaps Satan used extravagant language because he knew nothing less would give him a chance of success. But then Satan always has found hyperbole his rhetorical device of choice. How we love the sound, even as we suspect its truth. We're fortunate that the Word could withstand the lack of language.

If you or I were alone in this desert with only our guidebook as companion, our road maps and pilgrim charts, which, as you say, haven't done us a whole lot of good so far, I wonder how comforting the print would be. It's a version of the old saw: If you were trapped on a desert island, which books would you take? Huh. That's a question only printbound people could think up. After reading the nonprint text of that ancient church I was telling you about and experiencing the frustration of a sign that was useless as a sign until after the fact (it was not really visible until you faced it, which wouldn't happen except on the return trip, and who needed it then?) I'm not sure any book would do the job of keeping melancholia and madness at bay. And if reading wouldn't, neither would writing. Maybe we need the face-to-face interchange of words given and received to maintain who we are. And that makes me wonder about Adam and Eve, just as thinking about language made me wonder about Jesus in the wilderness.

What really happened in Eden? What did Adam and Eve lose that we are seeking, even in this desert? Wasn't it just that thing—the face-to-face interchange of words with God? They could talk to him, and did. They could talk to each other. They could talk to the animals too; I know they could. But after Eve listened to the hyperbole of Satan and Adam listened to Eve's linguistic imitation of the argument, then what? To be like God, which means, to a degree, the ability to mean something with language, to be able to talk to God and one another without distortion or ambiguity.

After they fell for Satan's words, they and we (and Satan himself, of course) use language to lie more often than we use it any other way. So the very thing Satan promised is the very thing we can never achieve; we've lost the face-to-face talk we long for. The Garden of Eden represents this ability to communicate without distortion, not, as we sometimes romantically think, as I have been guilty of thinking, a paradise of pleasant weather and beautiful pathways, the pilgrim's dream. No, Eden is something much more fundamental, for language is the core of who we are.

I suppose this language business also lies at the heart of how we pilgrims travel, not alone but in a company. We are a story-sharing breed. Leave it to cats and dogs (cats especially) to think profundities and inscrutabilities without talking about them; we, on the other hand, have a God-induced drive to talk about what goes on in our heads, even if what goes on is no more than a list of what we need at the grocery store.

And yet, when we're all done and have explained ourselves to a fair-thee-well, what have we accomplished? We may have cleared a small path from you to me, but the brambles still surround us. Those brambles make pilgrimage so difficult, whether it is a pilgrimage taken with words or with our feet. As I have been implying, pilgrims don't really choose between the two, for as we walk we talk, though sometimes the rigors of the path call a halt to our talk: We can't find the waymarks for the weeds. That's certainly an advantage to putting a red arrow high on a utility pole where few weeds can presume. When we spend our energy chopping weeds down to size to make a path passable, we have little left for talking or the trip. Another paradox. They're beginning to grow as rampant as the weeds themselves. We can't go if we can't get through the path, but once we've cleared the way we're too tired to move. At this point, I say bag the weeds, forget them, ignore them, brush them aside; let's get on with the trip. A few nettles never hurt anyone, at least not for long.

But haven't I violated the metaphor that I used at the beginning of a previous chapter? If the weeds are the circles we must necessarily run in—home, work, home, work—then how can we forget them to move ahead? There's a question ready-made for a guide, which, as we know, we haven't got, at least not physically, someone we can hand a cup of coffee to, lean across the kitchen table toward, look in the eye, and say, "Will you tell me where I'm supposed to be going? And how I'm supposed to get there given the bills I've got to pay? This isn't the year 1350, you know." Can we make our circles into straight lines? Or gentle curves, something that resembles a path? I should be able to answer my own questions, but I find myself inarticulate, mute, hoping that you have an answer, however tentative.

For these questions return me in proper circular fashion to my longing for the ancient rituals of walk and talk, a company of faithful witnesses to the deeds of the disciples, who themselves walked and talked all over the known world, regardless of the weeds they had to fight. It also puts me back to finding the road inside myself as well as finding the path with my feet. In the case of Bunyan's Christian he was headed for the Celestial City, an image of heaven, or Eden. Or does it matter? We're headed, in C. S. Lewis's terms, wherever the Master lives, the Lord of the country. Still, it would be comforting to have that face-to-face, over-a-cup-of-coffee conversation.

Travelers' Tales

....

I sometimes think pilgrims are of all people the most insecure, the most angst-ridden, the most in need of reassurance and comfort. Whatever I read tells me this truth, if I needed any confirmation other than my own eyes and ears, and yours. We walk with muscles shaking and bones quaking, even when we walk with others. We need companions on the trip so that we won't be forced to talk to ourselves. We need companions to tell our stories to—the delight of discovering how many ways people become pilgrims. We also need companions to share with each other the fears we have about the journey and our abilities. Who are we? Where do we belong? Why don't we fit? Can we make it up this hill? How long can we stop to rest without stopping dead? We need each other for *definition*.

When I find myself on certain paths, like the moors of Great Britain, especially those made infamous by Arthur Conan Doyle or Emily Brontë, some peculiar memories come to me. It would make sense if I said I relive—or reread, to continue what we began a few pages back—a story like *The Hound of the Baskervilles*. Yet not once has Doyle's detective come to my mind. Rather, I am constantly reminded of the Israelites, who created several generations of pilgrims by refusing to obey the Lord. I see those twelve tribes struggling up and down Two Moors Way; I hear their cries for help that arise out of the deepest despondency possible—the knowledge that their circumstances stem from their inability to accept the unknown that was all Yahweh was willing to offer. If the Israelites weren't insecure and angst-driven, then who has been?

I recognize the incongruity of such a vision, or at least the incongruity when I think back to Sunday school days. Wilderness. In my child's mind I equated it with desert. A barren, desolate, sandy place. The moors of Great Britain may be desolate, particularly in a mist, but they aren't barren or sandy. They aren't flat. Treachery, however, for the unwary walker, lies in every footfall. One of England's maximum security prisons was built in the moors because the terrain proved almost escape proof. Yet, ironically, I walk into an escape-proof land to find the way to escape the land I'm in.

If treachery lies before us, if this is *fundamentally* true for all pilgrims on all paths, is it any wonder that we walk with every confidence that our next step will land us in a bog or an old mine shaft? I remind myself of poor Puddleglum, the gloomy Marsh-wiggle in Lewis's Narnian tale *The Silver Chair*; no one was so confident of failure as Puddleglum, which, perhaps, is why he finally succeeded. That seems to be about the only confidence we can muster, the inescapable belief that we don't know where we're going. The Unknown is all we know.

I need to interrupt myself here, before you do, to ask myself why I am once again harping on the hardships? What about joy? Sunlight? The shared laughter over a pot of creamy Great Northerns spiced by garlic and onion at the close of a muscle-stretching day? Now is the time for stories, for reliving what you saw that I failed to notice or reminiscing about other walks, other meals, other companions and telling their stories as our own. Once I hear your story or that of someone you've known they become mine, stories I can share with subsequent companions. All that I've read I give to you, as you do the same for me. We double the joy immediately. Even the story of the Israelites, as miserable as its evolution, bears repeating if only for the drama of a people on the brink of failure or success. The poignancy of such words as, "If I forget thee, O Jerusalem, . . ." infiltrates our longing for place, a hunger for a city that both metaphorically and physically embodies the paths we profess. The passages of the Israelites become our paths, wherever we happen to walk. But again only in print.

I wonder what would happen if we wrenched the stories out of their cloth-bound worlds and recited them with rhyme, repetition, ritual, if we made them song and poetry, if we told and retold them to each other as we crouch beside our rock waiting for another sundown. What if this rock became the rock that Moses struck? What if this desert saw the Israelites trudge toward us? Of course, when we double the silence by reading the stories alone, to ourselves, out of hearing and touch of others who hunger for the sounds of true words, we remove their power another step or two. We've even reduced pulpit reading to a mere recitation of text—a verse, a few verses—which we all dutifully follow, holding the print in our hands. Again I wonder—what if the stories emerged from the community, one voice taking up the tale, then another, and another, reciting, and reenacting by reciting, the tales that make up the traditions of our faith. A community slipping into present tense, participating in the dialogue between Jesus and the rabbis. Isn't that the point of the Lord's Supper? Reenactment, remembrance, resurrection of the event as if it happens now, before us, for the first time, a tale to tell to our children and grandchildren.

No doubt the pilgrim way is treacherous. So was Jesus' walk to Golgotha. But the stories we own, the stories we are, fill the walk with joy and laughter and comfort, provided we share them with each other. Pilgrims can't be hoarders of anything—comfortable socks, ointments and bandages, or tales. I wish I knew why people in 1350, to circle back to that date again, understood the power of the exchanged word when we, who have more means to transmit the word than they dreamed of, leave it to the professionals. Radio and TV announcers. Critics. Preachers. People paid to pass on the word, any word.

So while we're surrounded by all kinds of talk—language of every sort—we ourselves find our vocal cords rusty from disuse, just as we would have in the Palestinian wilderness facing a razor-sharp tempter. We let others speak for us, or perhaps we just let others speak, not really caring whether they speak for us or against us. Words become fillers, like a public-service announcement in a magazine. They're nothing we need to attend to, because the words of professionals aren't our words and therefore lack meaning. We speak a vernacular that they can't understand, and they speak formulas we have no interest in learning. Because they don't tell our story, or the story of anyone we know in the way we know it and in the language we conceive of it, we have forgotten the excitement of exchanging words. One of us, either us or the professionals, suffers from illiteracy, the inability to use language, and on a trip time hangs heavy when we don't fill it with the language of shared experiences.

How terrible is silence—at times. It stretches above us, it encircles us, it keeps us from one another, an airbag gone haywire. So we're back to breaking the silence the wilderness imposes on us, retelling each other of the silences of other wilderness journeys to keep the silence at bay. The way the Jews retell the Passover fills the need of the people to know where they came from and why they're here. Some Christians have appropriated the seder for Maundy Thursday, a reenactment of the first Last Supper, for just that reason. We need to act the story of our roots. It's what drives me to the role of tenth-century worshiper. Once upon a time, I tell myself, once upon a time, pilgrims came here to hear why they were pilgrims.

Once more we face another paradox. How different are we from pilgrims who once put themselves into the hands of a priest who mediated the story of their faith? Don't our professionals do the same? Perhaps. But perhaps our professionals have forgotten the plot. Or they want to tell one story while we, gathered around in a circle, wait for "once upon a time." We don't want to hear about quarks and big bangs, as interesting and intriguing as those tales may be; as all children do, we want to hear about the time grandma and grandpa were little. If we are privileged to know our great grandparents then the stories improve with age. The farther back we can reach for our stories the better.

So we gather around the storyteller waiting to hear what time out of mind can bring us. We want the words *In the beginning. . . . Let there be light. . . . And it was good. . . . And then. . . . God created—us.* Naturally, that's the part of the story we love best. Each of us wants to be the hero;

each of us wants to be present at his own birth. It is a regret that though she is, she also isn't, because consciousness doesn't come with the first exterior breath. Writers as different as William Wordsworth and P. L. Travers, the creator of Mary Poppins, have shown us how much we wish we had been there, so to speak. We treasure evidences that connect us with the day we were born—a letter written on our nativity, a story told and retold.

Of course, as the original story goes, we will reach the part where we bungled it; retelling the tale inevitably leads us to the hard parts. Kicked out of the Garden, deprived of the face-to-face talk of the master talespinner. Reduced to partial hearing, partial sight. Forced to become pilgrims when we were made to live inside the story we're now trying to walk into. God thrust Adam and Eve into space and time; we might say that until they sinned time and space as we know those dimensions didn't exist.

When I write that we were made to live *inside* the story, I mean that we were made to live without just those dimensions that now give us so much trouble. Life with God, the face-to-face language we lack, meant life unbound by time and space, what Einstein called *chronotope*, space time. So now when we, as pilgrims, constantly confront chronotope in all its frustrations and limitations—all those circles that keep us spinning like a top out of control—because in some senses we are outside space and time, trying to get in. While we lived within Eden we lived in the center of chronotope, in the same center as God and so it exerted no binding force. Not that space and time didn't exist but that they existed as servant, not as master.

Several images come to mind when I try to conceive

of the liberation of Eden. I go to my stock of stories and hear my mother tell of the time she drove in the eye of a hurricane that suddenly struck Key West. Not until much later did she discover what she had done. From her perspective no storm existed, because she existed within it, on the inside. Those outside the storm struggled against its ferocity. In the same way, we are outside Eden and chronotope and so contend with it. Also in my stock of stories are those from the Old Testament, which describe God in just those terms, the center, the still point, or, in the terms of *this* story, the haven, the oasis. In a desert, such a space as we occupy, an oasis serves as the eye of the storm.

Yet we are no longer Edenites but pilgrims.

Recalling our flight from Eden into pilgrimage, I recall not just the Genesis account but that of John Milton, not a writer in good standing in our time. Feminists don't like him; teachers don't like him; students don't like him. Because his name conjures up all kinds of negative images, I mention him with hesitation. Yet when it comes to the story of our failures, the biblical account and Milton's *Paradise Lost* come together in my mind. Whether Milton intended that, I don't know, though the effect isn't that far removed from "justifying the ways of God to men," which he *did* say he wanted to do (maybe there lies our discomfort with him, because certainly that is a presumption not many of us would make).

Blind John Milton. I don't think I would have found him a very comfortable traveling companion. He wasn't easy to live with, a demanding, flinty man with an unforgiving brilliance. The fear of blindness must have tormented to him, as his beautiful sonnet "On His Blindness" allows us to glimpse. So, though I might have found him less than a comfort, I cannot do without the comfort of *Paradise Lost*. Somehow he was able to capture the joy of innocence and the sorrow of knowledge. It's a message we need, so voracious are we for knowledge, so unreflecting about the implications and responsibilities of knowing. John Milton makes me think about such matters.

Part of being a pilgrim is the need to retell, revisit, return, to interrupt and edit what we've done, to recall again and again where we've been and where we are and where we're going. Although we think we can't go back— people tell us often enough that we can't repeat the past—we can and do go back. With every retelling, revisiting, or rereading of what happened, with every rewriting, we change the past. Somehow it is always the same and yet never the same. History is only a story read and written by someone, and every he or she will read and write the same history differently. Theoretically we may be bound by the structures of events, but our dynamic memory, which is not tied to chronotope, allows us to pilgrim backward to reread and reinterpret those events. We are always inserting something new into the tale or recalling something we missed before.

Think about your family. Do your parents remember certain events exactly as you do? Much of the fun and frustration of family comes from just this fact of retelling the stories; each event is indeed a different event, depending on who tells it. You and I will tell different stories of our pilgrimage, you may be sure, just as my husband and I tell different stories of our walk through the Cotswolds to reach that tenth-century church. We might even tell different stories each time we repeat them, so that what I wrote several weeks ago, were I to write it today or tomorrow, might end up another tale entirely and yet still be the story of the same event. And each time we insert something new or delete something old comes the need for further correction and transition, for linking what we did before to what we do after, from one pilgrim turn to another. At the moment, the story is Eden— Genesis and John Milton. Which returns us to a blind guide no longer respected. How appropriate for this out-of-fashion enterprise.

It is no good thinking that pilgrims start out and head straight for the destination, just as I start out with page one and head straight for the end, fully conscious of where I'm headed and why. That's why an author's intention is at one level no good as a guide, be it John Milton's or any other author-pilgrim. Although a pilgrimage involves walking forward, more often than not it involves retracing our steps in order for us once more to pick up the path or to learn everything from the path we should have earlier. What have we left unexplored? What *must* we leave that way? What can we explore only later, in a different place on the pilgrim path, from a different perspective, from a different time?

Although many writers understand this, because somehow writing and pilgrimage share similar properties, none expresses it better or in more pilgrim terms than novelist Eudora Welty looking back at her journey into story. "It is our inward journey," she writes, "that leads us through time—forward or back, seldom in a straight line, most often spiraling. Each of us is moving, changing, with respect to others. As we discover, we remember; remembering, we discover; and most intensely do we experience this when our separate journeys converge." I read and copied this nearly two years ago. I found it recently, long after I had written about the spirals and circles we live in, only after I had written that we don't always follow a straight line. Again, I fall into insert mode, for here her journey and ours converge. We remember, we discover, we tell, we retell, we find our stories embodied in each other.

So when I leave my chair each day to encounter the vicissitudes of chronotope, I nevertheless take with me this pilgrimage of writing. Thus I experience several pilgrimages simultaneously, just as you do. Or are they merely parts of one great pilgrimage you and I and Eudora Welty are called upon to read, write, and live? A living text.

A living text. I must repeat those words, because they haunt me. I've heard them in such strange contexts, from an academic lecture hall—where speaker and Brown University professor Robert Scholes tells me that all life is reading, all life is writing, all life is text, that each of us is a living text—to the pulpit of my church and the pages of Paul's letter to Romans, which tell me that I am to be a living sacrifice, a living message, a living text. How can I hear from a disenfranchised Catholic the most holy of messages? How is it that he can remind me of what it means to be a pilgrim—a story told and retold, read and reread, a story lived? I have no answers. I only know that such is the way of pilgrimage, that along the way all sorts of people will remind us of what we are about.

So I ask, am forced to ask, *am* I a living text? What do people read in me? What am I writing me to be read *as?* Or is the author none other than Yahweh himself? These questions reveal levels and levels of pilgrimage that I did not see when I started and still am not prepared to answer. Yet it appears that when you and I said yes to the pilgrim call we committed ourselves to far more than we understood. A living text. And a pilgrim life to learn what writing and reading such a text means.

All this I take with me each day. And when I return to my chair I am forced to retrace my steps, paging back again and again, sometimes only a few pages, sometimes so far back that I page to the beginning, asking myself have I said it right? Are you and I reading it right? What would happen if we read it wrong? Is this pilgrimage or is it merely tourism? Are we part of Anne Tyler's book, *The Accidental Tourist?* Do we agree with the main character, Macon Leary, who insists that the goal of travel is to remain as insulated and isolated from others as possible? He wants no life-changing events. Or are we part of God's book, whose purpose is to disturb and disrupt our assumptions? I don't always know how to answer that question.

Sometimes I wish I could page forward to the finish, even though I know that nothing exists there yet, at least from my perspective. The privilege of paging forward belongs to God alone, though you and I long to know how this is all going to come out. Will we ever reach the Celestial City? Will we find Paradise Regained? Will we even find our way out of the desert? All the questions seem to come down to these: How will the story end? And when? The anxiety of the questions drives us to all sorts of strange speculations. Pilgrims should have enough with living the tale at hand without trying to live the tale ahead of time.

And yet, because we long to know the ending, we tell each other stories in which we know what happened, as if reassuring ourselves that our story will turn out the same, even in death. Such is the story of Adam and Eve, one whose plot seems to take a wrong turn, though embedded in it is the small promise that things will turn out all right. I call it small because unless we attend to the reading closely we might miss it—a throwaway line appropriate to comedy, since it portends restoration to more than tragedy and death. *Paradise Lost,* this retelling by John Milton, is part of my memory, a story I can tell and retell, for which I'm grateful, because there I *can* read the end, at least as Milton imagined it. He gives me Adam and Eve, heads bowed, hands clasped. Saddened, remorseful, accepting the consequences of their actions and fully knowing what they have brought to us, they become the first pilgrims.

When I write these words, I write from memory of the text and not from the text before my eyes. I could go get it. I could stop, walk up three flights, reach for my new, never-yet-opened, copy of *Paradise Lost* (I now own three), carry it down three flights, and open it to Book XII to read Milton's exact words. Yet I resist. I want to *remember* the story, not look at print. I want to read it in memory, to do with it what I wish churches did with Scripture. I want a living text; I want to live the text.

And I do resist the day I write these words. Days later, however, when I return to this page to reread what I find, I know that the need to read the exact words is stronger than my memory. Now, so many years later, do I understand all that my early Sunday school teachers told me when they made us memorize Scripture. I hear them intone what were then unintelligible words to me: "There are places in this world that do not have a Bible or any book at all." It wasn't a matter of disputing their assertion; I simply never entertained it, because the book-bound child that I was could not conceive such truth. Sometimes in order to hear the truth a person already needs to know it; so in my case. I knew nothing of non-book cultures. I knew nothing of people who live their stories instead of read them.

Had I memorized Milton along with Micah or Mark I wouldn't be forced to open my text. Nor would I need to decide where the ending begins or how far back to go to read what I paraphrase in my memory. Is it line 645, five lines from the finish, or line 641, where Adam and Eve look back on all that they lost, and lost us; do I page back even farther? In some senses, the ending occurs at the beginning, with one of the most famous sentences in all of literature, some fifteen lines long:

> *Of man's first disobedience, and the fruit*
> *Of that forbidden tree, whose mortal taste*
> *Brought death into the world, and all our woe, . . .*

This is followed by an almost equally long sentence that culminates in even more famous words: "And justify the ways of God to men" (25). As C. S. Lewis said of this opening, we know that some great thing is about to begin—indeed nothing less than human history, nothing more than God's promise of restoration.

The beginning here is the end, which reminds me that some storytellers define a novel as merely an ending postponed for as many pages as a writer can hold it off. Isn't that true of Adam and Eve? The inevitability of the fall strikes us forcefully, whether in Milton or in Genesis; our question is one of how long can they hold out, not *will* they. The opening lines propel us to the closing lines, so that again I want to read directly the fate of the first pilgrims. And now, at last, I do, some of the most beautiful lines ever written:

Some natural tears they dropped, but wiped them soon;
The world was all before them, where to choose
Their place of rest, and providence their guide:
They hand in hand with wandering steps and slow,
Through Eden took their solitary way.

The majesty of the opening gives way to the resignation sounded at the conclusion, a resignation with the hope and emblem of pilgrimage, when we travel together to seek what these two lost, with Providence as our guide.

John Milton isn't always easy to read, though these final lines seem to belie the impression we have of his density. Some of *Paradise Lost* is tough going for modern pilgrims better prepared to read snappy slogans than blank verse that marches stately on the page and in the mind. Our love of the short quip, the quick concept, makes us vulnerable to all those tourist ads we've been drooling over here in the desert. How could we fit Milton onto a billboard? His epic wouldn't make good copy for the four-color fantasies we hold in our hands, which whet my longing for a return trip to the gardens of Sissinghurst Castle.

I'm a true heir of Adam and Eve, always willing to believe the words of the wily serpent who offers easy-street tourism, because the ponderous words of obedience and fidelity take too long to get through. We're no longer a race that suffers slowness easily, whether in words or in people. It simply takes too long to reach the end of Milton, and even the end must be read by rolling the words on the tongue without haste. We want words that come easily and leave our mouths without making a mark, words that don't require our responsibility for them. But what kinds of conversations do such words produce? What kinds of pilgrimage would such language inform? Words that slip on and off the tongue seem more fitting for tourism than the trip we have undertaken.

Conversations. A communion of conversations, the giving and receiving of story. If I had never heard Milton's tale, how much richer I would be for having someone recite it to me now. Although I walked three flights to find the text, although I insisted on reading a few lines to myself, although I admitted that Milton was hard to read, I have not told the story true. Milton should be said, not read. Epic is, as with no other genre, oral. If we cling to its text in silence, we do it and ourselves a disservice, for it commands us to bring the words out into the open: Speak me, hear me, recite me, retell me. These are also the words of pilgrimage. Tell the story; don't keep it to yourself.

If our preface became "Remember the time . . ." what would happen? Of course, we need more than simply a willingness to remember the time and retell it; we also need a willingness to hear. Jesus was obliging in this business of storytelling, but not everyone was so obliging as to hear his tales. Just another rabbi in the parable-telling tradition. So exchanging stories, alternately listening and speaking, becomes another image of the community of pilgrims we are part of, past, present, and future, though here, now, we're interested in what others have experienced to help us through our own experiences.

It might bother some of us to seem so past-conscious, but to recall our stories and to give each other stories we can then retell is to inform the present and transform the future. The story you tell me helps me understand the circumstances of now; it may even determine my actions, which have future consequences I know nothing of at the moment. What better way to deal with time than through stories that put us into the center where, like the eye of the storm, time cannot touch us? Otherwise, our movement through time and space—our movement as the *result* of time and space—buffets us off the pilgrim path by making us focus on them and not on why we're walking. In the arrogance of the present and bereft of the past, we cut ourselves adrift in a space without context or root. And that is more difficult, more terrifying, than the hardest walk up the steepest hill to reach the narrowest path along the cliff edge with sea and rock below. It is akin to losing the path entirely.

When I think of such a path, my palms begin to sweat and my fingers begin to stick to my computer keys. I have acrophobia, a fear of heights. Lots of people do. As a pilgrim I will go lots of places so long as the places aren't high, narrow, or steep. That cuts out a good bit of walking, since the paths of pilgrims don't always fall on the broad way. So I had to relinquish my fear or forget the trip. I've climbed a lot of cliff edges that frightened me. Not that I would admit that to an inveterate walker who has braved the heights and desolation of Scotland, but in my context I've gone places I would never have dreamed I could navigate and would not had I thought about them before I set out. Which again shows the wisdom of the pilgrim principle: Start walking first, ask questions later.

In Great Britain, a stout walker can travel from the southwestern coast near the town that served as Thomas Hardy's model all the way to the northwest of Devon. Such a route would take a person around Land's End in southern Cornwall and up its coast until eventually the path turns right to head across north Devon. I don't know whether the path continues until a walker might turn left again and move north for Wales. But why borrow trouble? The path I'm sure of makes for prodigious pilgrimage. Not that I have walked this coastal path of hundreds of miles, though someday. . . .

I have managed bits of it—fifteen- to twenty-mile stretches. Some of the paths are child-simple, two feet broad and grassy or hard-packed earth. Others are little more than sheep trails; in fact, they are sheep or goat paths, those fellow-pilgrims on British soil. Since my feet are wider than animal hooves, such trails can be tricky, particularly in pouring rain. Looking for shelter on a path where to your left is an immediate and steep descent to rock and sea below (there go my palms again) and nothing much but inclines of impervious, chewing sheep to the right makes a pilgrim think that sometimes there's nothing to do but keep going. Maybe the rain will let up soon. However, if a pilgrim wants authenticity, if a pilgrim wants the path to make her think of other pilgrims and other paths, then this is the way to walk. I don't think so well of pilgrimage sitting in comfort—or just sitting, for that matter. Something about the walk moves me to consider just what I am about. I am never more connected with the pilgrim life we're called to than when my knees hit my nose as I head up a rocky path.

As I write, I return to the coast of Cornwall and a dreary summer day more reminiscent of a Midwestern March than June. We were staying in north Devon on the edge of Exmoor outside a town called Combe Martin in twelfth-century Holdstone Farm of mostly sheep: shearing all week. We learned that each kind of sheep fleece had to be wrapped, bagged, and labeled separately, a job that takes days and several people. Sheep-farming is, in its own way, as labor intensive as dairy farming; the rhythm of the work is merely different. But no farming is easy, as we had reaffirmed in all parts of the country.

From Combe Martin on the coast to North Cornwall is not far by U.S. standards, perhaps an hour-and-a-half drive from Tintagel (pronounced, as I remind myself, tin-TA-jel; nothing so disturbs people than to have their names mispronounced, even place names). Our friends had insisted that if we were anywhere in the vicinity of Tintagel we had to visit it. I have read tales of King Arthur since I was young, and though there may be some I have overlooked, I doubt it. And yet I did not recollect Tintagel, the site of the ruins of a sixth-century castle—we were moving backward in history—the supposed birthplace of King Arthur. Merlin figured in the legend too, as he always does, for below the castle is Merlin's cave, the one we read about at the end of the Arthur story. "Make sure you visit the cave," our friends had urged. "Bring me back a rock," requested one.

Tintagel has something about it of a holy site, the British equivalent of those American ones I mentioned earlier on this journey, Graceland or Disney World. But with what a difference: a castle more than a thousand years old, some of the stone walls still standing at the head of the inlet, a high promontory, imposing its authority still on all that surrounds it—pasty shops and potters alike. King Arthur, Merlin, the Knights of the Round Table, Guinevere, Lancelot, Gawain, Mordred, all such familiar names, names and stories that have influenced numerous writers.

Leaving the narrow, nearly tourist-like streets to

climb toward the castle is to drop back into ancient memory, a memory I had nourished by the rhythms of my reading: Mary Stewart, T. H. White, Marion Bradley Zimmer, Susan Cooper, Sir Thomas Malory. Even people who have never heard of those writers have heard of King Arthur, such is the force of legend. Was Arthur a Christian king? Or did the Druids still hold the people? What is true, what false in what we know of the man? What is it about the Arthur story that still leads people to search for him? Why did I find the tale so fascinating?

In this tale of pilgrimage, churches may be one thing, but rubble-stubble castles of problematic historical figures surely are another. No wonder that those this side of the Protestant Reformation, like those this side of the Gutenberg revolution, are suspicious of the words pilgrim and pilgrimage, since for some of us they conjure up just such images as I have been writing about—myth, legend. Read the word *falsehood*. Pilgrims and pilgrimages can so easily go wrong; even those in the Catholic tradition find visits to holy places difficult to assess, perhaps because of our definition of *holy* and of *place*. Perhaps, too, because of what we think such journeys will bring. Is it salvation we seek? Holiness? Miracles? A touch of the divine? And what do these questions mean? We have an uneasy relationship with the notion of being a pilgrim, despite the quintessential Protestant writer John Bunyan, whose best efforts show us that life is simply that—a pilgrimage. Yet even he admits that we can get it wrong, that we can *go* wrong, despite the directions we have in hand.

We also have suspicions about pilgrimage because so many other religions make it central—devouts must make a pilgrimage. Practitioners of Islam automatically come to mind. A visit to a sacred stone smacks of paganism; and so too could a visit to any place we designate as sacred or meaningful, even a visit to our local church on Sunday, if we somehow misrepresent it as the-thing-itself and not merely a sign or an image.

But Bunyan reminds us that we can view life itself as a pilgrimage, not merely see pilgrimage as an event that occurs once or twice during our lives. And that, perhaps, may be the difference between this view of pilgrimage and another, that the end of the journey occurs within the journey, that all along Bunyan's hero, Christian, embodied the path; it was inside him as well as outside him.

How many times had I traveled to Tintagel, without even knowing its existence? I had read so many tales of King Arthur that his story had become part of my memory, almost as if what had happened to him had happened to me. I willed him to exist, if not in all the details, because from Malory on the details had shifted under the hands that wrote the tales. Our trip in the car was a long, internal journey as well as a brief, external one, this time connecting me with another sort of history, yet one not dissimilar from the history I became in the Cotswold church. There I participated with pre-print worshipers; in Tintagel too I found pre-print peoples caught in a struggle between pagan worship and a rudimentary notion of Christianity; at least, that is the tale I chose to appropriate.

The irony is that such an ancient struggle is not all that dissimilar from the struggle we live each day of our pilgrimage. It might even have been easier for Arthur than for us, because the line between pagan and Christian is so blurred today that we find it hard to distinguish; sometimes I think there is no distinction so that we have returned full circle to the early church fathers who decided to appropriate and Christianize pagan rites for the faith. It seems only inevitable now that paganism has turned around and appropriated Christian rites to itself. I began with one such rite, Advent, and have written us into another, Lent, the two pivotal seasons of the Church year, the two pivotal seasons of the pagan year.

Writing into Lent. That phrase occurred to me as I listened to a sermon about Abraham, who made a painful pilgrimage to sacrifice his son. I had never before read that pilgrimage from Isaac's perspective. What kind of pilgrimage was it for him? It isn't every day that a father ties up his son and takes a knife to his throat. Surely Isaac struggled and screamed, despite the sad-eyed pictures we find in our Bibles, a romanticized, compliant Isaac, as romanticized as any tale of King Arthur and probably as unrealistic. Yes, the Church reads Isaac as a type of Christ (sometimes even King Arthur is read that way), but Jesus didn't go to the grave easily, despite how we romanticize that story, that Lenten story.

Both the story of Gethsemane and the story of Isaac's escape from the knife read and write me into Lent. All along we have been Lenten bound, inexorably moving us toward the triumph and death of Jesus, inexorably moving us toward our own death. But not yet. Jesus, first; we'll get to our own soon enough. Such knowledge shows again how many pilgrimages we partake in simultaneously—reading, writing, walking, reliving, reenacting first this story, then another, all stories seeming to meet at the foot of the final great story.

It's sometimes difficult to realize that every story we read and recite occurs in another context than itself, or in another context than the one in which we find ourselves when we finally reach it and read. What, I often wonder, was the context—or more exactly the contexts—of the story as originally conceived? I long to know the time and the place when the original was written, the time and the place when the writer became the reader to discover what the writer had written. I also long to know the time and the place when another reader picks up the book to recreate the text I have written. I try to imagine it, the time of year, the psychological state of my reader, the material circumstances. Writers and readers come together in a social union, just as surely as do people who meet and talk. The layers upon layers of our pilgrim lives inform what we write, whether we write as living texts for others to read or print-bound texts intended for a, perhaps, different kind of reading.

So I partially answer my question: I write from Advent into Lent, a journey of just a few months that symbolizes a lifetime. We need to write into and through the inevitable story begun when Adam and Eve walked slowly through the gates of Eden into time and history. From that event all else follows, even my trip to Tintagel, which I write as Lent draws to a close and remember as part of Pentecost, the celebration of the coming of the Comforter.

And here we find an oasis in our desert. It is a good place to stop.

Pitfalls

···

I pick up the thread of Tintagel and like Theseus in the labyrinth feel my way along its slight diameter back to the day and time when I encountered Cornwall. What, I wonder, lies at the heart of my maze? Shall I find a Minotaur?

A slight tug on the thread reassures me that I am on the path to Tintagel, and, yes, I see crowds of cows on land that is becoming increasingly Merlin-like. Today, we think, few people will risk the weather, but we have learned that even on the remotest path we invariably run into inveterate walkers, intrepid, irrepressible. My thread winds into Cornwall, through a few villages, and so to the Cornish coast and the castle, where it ends. High tide prevents us from joining Merlin in his cave; an entrance fee keeps us from crossing the castle threshold. We stand below at the gate and watch others circle and circle to reach the door. Stonehenge taught us that sometimes the greater view is outside, not within where perspective is foreshortened. Structure and purpose often become invisible to those inside, which is the reason we find ourselves at a loss to determine our structure, our purpose, except by listening to those outside ourselves who read us more clearly than we can ever hope to read ourselves. Yet, paradoxically, only by penetrating the circle can we participate in what it portends. I could not join the invisible Cotswold worship unless I sat where generations of pilgrims sat; so perhaps I miss my opportunity to join the Arthurian company by hanging on to my pound fifty. Nevertheless, this day we choose to separate from the circle.

Then had we journeyed from Combe Martin to Cornwall for nothing? We turn from our left and the castle toward the sea. An odd picture comes to mind, oil rigs in the North Sea, even rougher and more treacherous than the sea Tintagel confronts. I see what we must conquer in order to fricassee chicken in vermouth and wild mushrooms and heat the kitchen simultaneously. No warmth radiates from the castle, even threading back to the sixth century when all the walls still stood. How much North Sea oil, I wonder, would it take to heat that stone? How many women working diligently with needle and wool did Tintagel need to drape the walls with warmth and, incidentally, with beauty? My thread has become entangled, I fear, among the stones of history. Did the sixth century warm itself with something other than animal skins?

Perhaps because I only come to stone in the cold, I always sense its chill. Yellowed Cotswold cathedrals seem warmer than the grayed and weathered stone in other parts of the country, though I know this is illusion. Even in heat does stone radiate cold, if that is possible. I'm glad to know this, however, as I move between sight of sea and stone, for it helps me understand the trappings of the priesthood that Protestants find so pompous. Necessity drives the purveyors of Grace to adopt their layers of intercession. I see these men moving up the rocky path, circling closer to the castle door; I see processions of priests, barely literate themselves, walking the treacherous coastal path to bring the word and food of grace to people who do not yet understand their need for either. They mingle with those I see before me, when I turn half-left from the sea, those who still fail to understand the hunger that drives them to such a place on such a day. Only the clothes have changed.

How would Britain's first missionary respond to find his work deconstructed, with only pockets of faith in the fabric of late paganism? All this is fancy, or *phantastie* as writers of sixteenth-century pilgrimage might spell it: None of it is real, this imaginative juxtaposition of mine. But as Eudora Welty writes, "Travel itself is part of some larger continuity." For you and for me, as I've suggested, our travel in these pages partakes of the larger pilgrimage, beginning with Eve and her spouse and without end, because we cannot page forward.

So if we choose to remain apart this day, pilgrims, not tourists, why do we come? Why does the thread I hold so gingerly lead me back to Great Britain's ancient history? I see the answer when I turn right to face the Cornish coast heading north to Wales and Scotland: massive outcroppings of rock and cliff carved by ocean and time. Can we reach the sand of some inlet, or is the stone too steep for trust? In the thinning mist we make out another kind of thread, this one quite physical, though no less narrow in diameter, a path along the cliff edge. To reach it requires returning to the bridge across the jetty, which will put us on the right side of *this* inlet, on whose left we still stand at the ticket gate, a nightmare of anachronism in such a setting.

We have a choice, I recall, as all pilgrims do who face

numerous paths. Further south down the coast is a cattle show that tempts us, while we also consider the cost of the sea cliff path. One takes us back to the car, the other keeps us on our feet. How high is the wind? I wonder, my phantasie filling with recollections of Sir Walter Scott and numerous gothic heroines cloaked in coarse brown and fighting to keep their footing.

The gatekeeper, seeing our hesitation, or bored, or impatient with our refusal to enter or leave, offers us help, this day becoming a guide, if only to point us where to walk and not to lead us there. "Avoid the cattle show." His imperative syntax left us in no doubt that traffic jams and irritation lay to our south. "You'll never get across the bridge into town," he added. "Four hours I waited once." Unlike *our* rural residents, Britain's backbone never hesitates to give advice, even if we don't always take it or even understand it.

But can we walk the path? Is it safe?

"Safe enough for experienced walkers." The gatekeeper-cum-guide eyes us suspiciously, taking in our stout boots, heavy socks, muscular legs, rain gear, and day packs. We bear his scrutiny, grateful that our boots show the scuff marks of numerous rocky climbs, and his suspicion yields to favorable judgment.

What about the beaches? Can we climb down or merely along the cliffs? Now I was the suspicious one. From where I stood I saw little in the way of safety or shelter should the need arise. As a guide giving advice the gatekeeper was good, but he would be huddled in his hut while we were searching for rocky shelter.

"Got my first child just there." He nodded vaguely toward a beach some miles distant. "Warmer than now, though." Another addition, succinct but important to the story. Although we already knew that the Cornish were hardier than most people of our ken, it relieved us to know that they weren't entirely beyond our reach.

"Also low tide. Today tide won't go out for hours." His eyes told us that he read the tide tables *in* the sea, where all coastal people find their text—not in print, like inlanders. My years of living along the coast of Connecticut had never taught me such reading, but I could see down the coast how little land the sea left exposed; I could look down at the mouth of Merlin's cave and watch the sea wash it; I could imagine the trap for those who little realize how quickly the sea comes in once it has a head of steam up. Hadn't I read enough stories where that figured into the plot?

"Fine walking, that." Again he nodded at the coastal path. "In any weather, though you can't see as far today."

We liked his speech, fragments though they might look on the page. His syntax carried completion, and that is all we should ask of language or people when we look for the next path on the pilgrimage.

In his language and in the path he preferred, we read a reason we had come—not for Arthur, not for Merlin, not for ancient tales of mythic Tintagel or burial caves. We had come for Cornwall itself, to put beneath our feet a living text, this narrow Cornish path. It represented, at least for that day, a desire to find some place of rootedness, where time went back a long time. It represented a longing for Eden and understanding that ultimately neither Cornwall nor any earthly place could satisfy: a loss-of-self to, paradoxically, find the self— beyond self, beyond death. If only death didn't stand as the way.

We could see that fighting weeds would not be the

challenge on this journey, for as far as the eye could see the path hardpacked its way along open cliff country with merely some shortcropped grass courtesy of grazing goats and sheep. Where we lost sight of the line the path moved down and around, following the sharp edges of the land. This path, we saw, would permit single file only.

Assured that the danger was not great, we repositioned our packs and made our way back to reach the foot of the path and so began our climb. What had seemed an insignificant incline from the perspective of the gate to Tintagel became quite another thing in reality. Which just goes to show, I thought, how little we understand of pilgrimage before hitting the trail. The path never looks as hard or as narrow ahead of time. We might have learned this lesson in the desert, walking and walking to reach a rock that seemed so short a distance from us. We *might* have. But it's in the nature of pilgrims to need to relearn our lessons with every path we approach.

On this Cornish path we found loose stone as well as stone embedded in the earth, the jagged edges making the rough path rougher, forcing us to take the path slowly and carefully. With heavy boots, a stubbed toe is insignificant unless it causes a pilgrim to trip. With a steep drop to my left and the narrow path beneath, I did not intend to risk a fall.

When on such a path, a pilgrim has little choice but to watch where she walks. I longed to look out over the sea and lose myself in it, to project myself over it and imagine I could make out the American continent. Such fancies, though, are only for times of rest, not for times of walking. I had to keep my eye on the path to stay on the path; imagination is one thing, the reality of the ocean quite another: They needed to remain separate.

We had experienced so many paths that had nothing in common except their difference. Walking the Cornish coast revised my notion of path. Or perhaps I finally understood the New Testament definition. I thought about the kinds of paths I usually traveled. Four-lane highways, eight-lane highways: broad, smooth, fast. Even the two-lane highways of town with their late-winter potholes are easy streets compared with the Cornish coast. I'd been on some paved paths that stated "unfit for motors," only to be forced into the brush a few minutes later by an Austin. But walking the sea cliffs I knew I would not run into that hazard. If this is what Jesus meant about broad paths and narrow paths, no wonder most people choose the former. No wonder, too, that pilgrims who choose narrow paths often tire and turn back. If we weren't avoiding some treacherous rock, we were avoiding the fresh evidence of sure-footed sheep. Much of the path, too, was up, great for strengthening thighs and building lung capacity; but paths curve down, eventually, just when we think we've conquered the hard part. Then we discover that the hard part has only begun, especially if the descent is long.

On this day on this path we did find ourselves walking into shelter of sorts, where the trail left the open-fielded top to make its way along rock ledges. When we looked down we saw beach that tempted us to find our way over the rock face to its level, but warning signs left little doubt that we could not reach the beach. Sometimes the signs said DON'T, at other times CLIMB AT YOUR OWN RISK. John Bunyan's Christian could have used such sign posts; so could most of us. But we've only been assured that the path is hard, not that it comes with labels to help us along the way.

I was beginning to wonder whether we had trusted our guide at the gate too readily; having been hungry for some guide we went with the advice of the first one we'd found, though why we took his word puzzles me. Could it have been the accent Americans are such suckers for— any and all that come under the rubric "British?" (The subtle class distinctions of accent escape most of us.)

It wasn't merely that the path was narrow. It wasn't merely that the path was steep. It wasn't merely that the path was taking us closer and closer to the edge of *terra firma*. It wasn't, even, merely that the rock hovering above us, rock we could touch for stability, was slippery. No. None of those facts made me wonder whether we had misplaced our trust, for they weren't, in the nature of such a walk, entirely unexpected. Rather, it was the iron boxes we kept finding. Iron boxes painted fire-engine red. Large, sturdy, imposing boxes, property of the Cornish coast guard or some such organization—let's call it, since my memory refuses to reread the letters painted in white and my journal holds no clue, the Cornish Rescue Service.

These rescue boxes embedded in the rock warned me that this path was more dangerous than our chosen guide had led us to believe. Why else would they be so frequent or contain such stout rope? Is it merely imagination that insists each one also held a telephone connected to Emergency headquarters, wherever that might be? What good rope would do I couldn't see. Should a pilgrim take a plunge to the rocks of sharks' teeth below a bit of rope, even as much a bit and as stout a bit as the sturdy boxes held, would be too little too late.

That's how I read the rope while on the path. But rereading my first frightening sight of what surely happened often enough to warrant the frequency of rope and boxes I now see that the rope wasn't for the preservation of life but the retrieval of death. As a way of reaching the rocks below in relative safety, the rope had a purpose. *Then* I imagined myself desperately chucking rope after Allen, knowing the futility of such action. (Remember how I hate heights, this reminder merely to show how phobias can fever the imagination of someone who probably read too many gothics as a child. Notice too that Allen, not I, in this story of mine was the foolish one to fall: maybe gothics serve some purpose.) *Now,* I imagined a different scene, one in which I wait for someone to rescue what remained, hoping he or they would arrive before the high tide took care of the details.

A gruesome tale? Inappropriate in this text? Another anachronism with the early century of Tintagel when neither rescue nor retrieval was possible? Our presence in such a place is no more anachronistic than that bit of rope. And that bit of rope is no less a metaphor for the pilgrim path for all that it is anachronistic.

I wrote that the rope could not possibly serve to rescue someone from danger—yet in a way its mere presence did just that. We have a way of becoming cocky, self-assured. What's another narrow path, a few more rocks below showing through the headfoam of the sea? Cornwall, Devon—what difference did it make? Hadn't we reached a beach on the Devon coast by using a rope for the last few feet, the ladder having rotted from years of seawater? Hadn't I nearly conquered my fears of such paths, so that now I was not paralyzed by its demands?

My palms still sweat when I remember, such is the physiology of phobia. And this remembering brings back the text of another, even more dangerous, pilgrimage that occurred when I was a teenager, an experience I'll never forget, despite the fact that I rarely remember it, because it returns to me at odd moments of reading or rereading other confrontations of pilgrim life. Spelunking (for those unfamiliar with the term, the e is long, the accent on the second syllable) is subterranean pilgrimage, the kind evil fairy-tale dwarfs go in for, not elves or people. It's not a pilgrimage for those who experience claustrophobia as I embody agoraphobia. Closed-in places have never bothered me but once or twice, convincing me that anyone can be overcome by any phobia given the right circumstances. My spelunking career—which began and ended one spring Sunday afternoon in Pennsylvania—was not shortened by claustrophobia but my fear of heights, my downfall once again.

My best friend attended a church with a young, adventuresome minister, a hypnotist and a spelunker, though not at the same time, of course. He knew of some interesting caves not that far a drive from our area, caves he himself had explored. Would the youth group like to go? Of course the youth group would like to go. Such was his influence that the youth group would have gone anywhere he suggested. I, as an honorary member of that group by virtue of my friendship with Carolyn, went as well. Not only was it my first and last caving, it was also the youth group's, for the caves were far more treacherous than we novices had any right to expect or business exploring. The minister had made a mistake, which nearly proved disastrous.

When I close my eyes and revisit that day, several scenes return clear and strong. One is crawling, or rather wriggling, flat on my stomach for long stretches, all of us in single file. Even so our heads scraped the roof of the cave, and the sides of our bodies touched rock left and right. Some kids couldn't take it and called retreat almost immediately. Here my memory fails—always, of course, at crucial points. Because now I want to know how they got out. There was no way to turn around. Did they back out? Or wait for an open space, then turn around? We did reach such spaces, though seldom. For the most part we wriggled, with an occasional break when we could crawl on our hands and knees.

So that is one scene of this drama. Reliving it I am frightened, nearly in panic at the thought of subjecting myself to spelunking again and shocked that I ever did so. This is not the sort of pilgrimage that promotes companionship, despite Tolkien's attempts to make caving attractive. Then I recall that in *The Lord of the Rings* Gandalf lost his life in a cave, being dragged by the Balrog into one of earth's potholes, which many caves have. His experience and mine meld in my memory, so that now for the first time I understand part of my fascination with that Middle Earth prose epic and the company of the Nine.

For the next scene I fastforward my videotape, having no recollection between flat-out belly work and standing at the edge of this cave's pothole, knowing that we couldn't tell bottom, no matter how we strained to hear the plunk of the stone we dropped. I knew that across the narrow ledge was the last bit of the journey, and it was either cross to daylight or return. We'd already been hours longer than we were supposed to have been. As I said, the minister made a mistake. I knew I had to do what others had done and cross that space. That open, forbidding height. That narrow ledge made wider by the feet of several guys who clung to the upward surface of the cave, forming a human bridge. I'd watched others cross with the nonchalance of someone going with the traffic light at a street corner in town. But I couldn't. I couldn't. Had I known Tolkien's tale, which I didn't read until years later, I might be standing there still, convinced that one step would surely be a misstep and that a Balrog was waiting below.

Something is missing in this part of the video, something that propelled me forward. I don't know how I began one of the longest journeys in my life, but I do know that I stopped halfway. If this is what Jesus meant by putting your hand to the plow and looking back, then I understand it. No one can move forward while looking in the opposite direction, not if she hopes for a straight furrow. But I'm mixing my metaphors again. This wasn't a study in farming techniques; this was a matter of survival, mine and the people whose feet I stood on. Stood stock still, to use a stock phrase. Stock, a stock, stockade, wood, enclosure, immovable, locked into one position. That tells it all. I stood there and could not move. Not forward. Not backward. And the grip of one part of the human bridge was slipping. Into the pit.

I know that people were talking to me, telling me to move. Telling me not to be afraid. Telling me I was almost there. I see it, as in a dream where I am the dreamer as well as the object of my dream. Yes, there I am, in the dark cave, standing on someone's foot, probably Phil Roth's. I'm chiselled there, while around me I see language bouncing off me like birds against plexiglass. Thud. Thud. The words drop dead. They can't get through, because my fright has shifted me beyond the grace of language. When that happens, as it sometimes does to all of us, we know that the Balrog has won; falling is irrelevant.

One word reached me, one voice—the minister's.

"Move!" Or was it two words? "Cheryl, move!" The imperative, syntax most languages have. I want to remember that he used my name, rather than the optional subject understood. But I don't remember anything except that I heard those words, obeyed the command, and reached the other side in safety. Did I argue? Did I whimper? I don't know. My video shows me nothing, except my safe arrival into sunshine. Blurred images cause me to hit the fastforward button once again. There I sit, black against bright, on the hood of a car, waiting for the rest to exit the earth. I have never been so earth-covered, not even when I revelled in mud baths as a toddler. If I had not been so relieved to have the air above me, I might have worried more about my mother, who was as angry as I could have predicted. I was hours late. I was filthy. I had ruined my clothes. Yes, the minister made a mistake.

I won't bother to rewind the video. Hit the eject button, pop out the tape, reshelve it. That incident after all has nothing to do with Tintagel or the cliffs of Cornwall, cliffs, not caves. The sea has seen to that. Yet the two memories, so far apart in time and space, superimpose themselves on one another, like a Dali painting, so that I view one through the scrim of the other, giving both incidents surrealism, distortion. Which probably makes both more realistic by being more surreal.

I am not one to take chances. I don't try to beat trains at railroad crossings; I don't lean out over the edge of life. Yet at least twice, I realize, I have placed myself, or allowed myself to be placed, in danger. To switch from one expression to the other is to deny my responsibility. The first time, of course, I *was* not entirely responsible, having no experience of spelunking so that I had to trust our guide. On the Cornish cliffs, although we accept the advice of a guide, I am in charge of what I do on the path. To be honest, however, once I agreed to go spelunking, I was responsible for how I accomplished the adventure. Had I not made it across that chasm, someone—my mother, the church—might have held the minister responsible, and I would not have been able to set things right by saying how wrong I was to panic. Now if I am foolish and refuse the guidance of warning signs, no one is to be faulted but myself.

Well, that's not right either, for that is an anti-pilgrimage statement. Pilgrims are part of a community and that by definition means we hold each other accountable; we bear each others' burdens. We're responsible for ourselves and yet not responsible at all. It seems that in this labyrinth of paths called the pilgrim way we inevitably reach yet another truth that defies logic, leaving us with a choice to admit into our fellowship the seemingly contradictory, or to refuse it outright, as Descartes and his disciples refused to admit paradox into their notions of mathematics. I don't know which it is, but for today I am willing to walk with the contradictions beside me.

On the Cornish cliffs, if I walk too fast, or too nonchalantly, I might make a mistake. I don't intend to. Probably the minister hadn't intended to, either, a voice prods me. I think, "Some mistakes we can't correct, no matter how many sorries we say." I don't want to be forced to abandon the path because of something I have done that I cannot undo; neither my life nor my computer provides me such an option.

All this I think as I study the fire-engine red box with its white words lighting the true road. Or I think of such matters now in remembering the Cornish coast and our halfhearted attempt at one point to find a way from top to bottom. I was the halfhearted part. No number of we-can-do-its would budge me from the ledge and my box of safety.

Whether our bickering brought them up from the sea at that moment, or whether, like a tree that falls in the forest with no one to hear, they would have arrived at that space at that time anyway, we learned again that no path is so remote that someone hasn't been there before us. I close my eyes against my computer screen, twitch my thread that now has turned into a hefty rope, and see again those two people, male and female, winding up the stairs, circling up, strolling up, hands on the guardrail— another feature of the Cornish rescue squad I had forgotten until these two shifted my eyes from their faces, down their neck and shoulders, and so to arms, hands, and fingers. Yes, clearly, I see a black iron rail. Allen's eyes flick me a sentence or two: *They* did it. *They* got down and up again. Just hang on to the rail. My eyes refuse his words and the consequences that reading would bring. I cannot explain my reluctance that day to adventure to the beach, when I had traveled down to Wild Pear Beach only a few days before. The exotic name must have overcome my hesitation. Here the situation was different—a beach whose path I could not see.

But what I could see troubled me. Usually when we meet people on remote trails we exchange a few words, often in the form of questions. This pair, however, did not encourage such pilgrim talk, for they seemed as startled as we to have met anyone on such a day in such a place. What I recall most clearly is the woman—a late teenager, really—her hair stringing down her back, wet from mist and rain, and her thin, hot-pink flats. How could she have climbed down and up such terrain in those shoes? I looked down at my own feet. Deep-treaded mountain climbing boots, waterproofed inside with Gortex and outside by a special paste (my feet still got wet—how I'll never understand, my right foot, especially), padded and reaching high above my well-protected ankles. I also wore two pairs of socks, a thin pair of polypropylene liners and a heavy pair of rag socks over them. I looked at the muscles I had earned and the sturdiness of my lean hiking legs. Then I looked again at this pale girl in pink shoes, legs bare and obviously unaccustomed to exertion. What sort of person was she to attempt the Cornish coast so unprepared?

Of course I have no way of answering my questions, for as I said they weren't interested in the reciprocity of tales, unlike others we had met on the trail, others who like us were pilgrims, at least of a sort. Here were tourists who had stumbled out of their element and into ours; only a tourist would trip down those cliffs shod in tropical pink. What was there to exchange? They had for a morning ventured off their predetermined path and could risk a few sore muscles, since the next day would not find them on such a trail again. We, on the other hand, would find another such trail, connecting us to another such ancient race as Arthur and Merlin and Tintagel. We couldn't afford to spend all our strength in one detour, even one that promised such a dramatic sight of the open water and the cliffs behind and above us as this Cornish beach did. Even though to appreciate the imposition of Tintagel on the land was to see it from the perspective of the sea.

Giants

....

"It is quite clear," says Don Quixote to his sidekick Sancho Panza, "that you are not experienced in this matter of adventures." Such utter conviction. Such total superiority. Such foolishness, thinks Sancho Panza. The irascible, illogical Don thinks the same of his sidekick. Two views of reality converge and conflict, two moral and philosophical positions on life. Don Quixote is not of the monastery but of the road; that much is obvious from—

But wait. Before I continue with that pilgrim who has been sentimentalized in quintessential Broadway show-tune fashion, I'd better give the context—for context, as we've been discovering, is all-important, whether we are reading or walking. Broadway has exchanged the original context of the Don—the Bohemian, the rogue, what some writers call the *picaro*—for one in which he "dreams the impossible dream." He is a subversive, a renegade, a counterculture figure transformed into another Horatio Alger. The Broadway Don does not have the values of the picaro but of the American Way of Life.

The character Miguel de Cervantes created in the seventeenth century never, but never, would sing such a sappy song. So if we think only of Don Quixote as a man with his head in the clouds, or in the sand, who fights unbeatable odds and who works with unbeatable courage, we don't know the Don at all. This is no bootstraps hero, the American nobility. Don Quixote has nothing sentimentally right or righteous about him, though there may be plenty of plain good sense in his reading of the world. Plain good sense with panache, of one who is used to a world that is not what it seems, a man who knows a metaphor when he meets one, no matter how literal-minded everyone else, even sidekicks, might be.

And of course, that is the situation here. The Don sees giants, Sancho Panza doesn't; the two worldviews in conflict. Don Quixote pushes Sancho Panza's worldview beyond the bounds that he is able to follow. Actually, Quixote dismisses them as irrelevant because he knows that things aren't always what they seem. So at the start of one of the most famous passages in all literature he says, "It is quite clear that you are not experienced in this matter of adventures." Here is the rest: "They are giants, and if you are afraid, go away and say your prayers, whilst I advance and engage them in fierce and unequal combat."

Now I can finish what I started earlier. The Don is for the road, the one essential element in the pilgrim worldview; he rejects the monastic life when he sends Sancho Panza to his prayers. The Don sees things only in black and white, which has its drawbacks. Some people walk and act, others pray, but seldom does one person do both. We, however, are on an unusual pilgrimage, and so for us the way of the road and the way of prayer merge and become one. Yet in Quixote's context, we admit that there may be something to his view.

Nevertheless, we find Don Quixote so ludicrous that the idea of looking foolish has become synonymous with a certain cast of pilgrims, the *picaresque*. Yet the Don is at the same time charming, a grown man engaging windmills, which of course would be unequal combat, for how could a man win? The odds are better with giants. Which, of course, is the point. They *are* giants, and if only Sancho Panza had been more experienced, he would have known this.

This puts us, once more, up against the circular, for a windmill is simply another kind of circle, those circles we've been fighting all along, only now we know they are giants, which puts the whole enterprise of pilgrimage on another footing entirely, as Don Quixote understands. We can't win, he can't win—yet we've no choice but to advance and engage them, laughing at the ridiculous situations we get ourselves into because we see giants when everyone else sees windmills.

Maybe I'm speaking only for myself here. I confront numerous giants every day where conflict—battle—and peace negotiations seem to be the order. Is the environment, or censorship, or letting my children listen to rap music a giant worth fighting? Sometimes it's difficult to decide. Each pilgrim must figure out which difficulty is a windmill, which a giant. I've known people to decide that obtaining a window office is a giant to be encountered. I recall a time when I thought so. Now that I've shifted countries, from business to education, I'm grateful for a desk and two chairs, one for me, one for a student: windmills not giants.

Perhaps the ability to appear ridiculous, to be content with a windowless office when others demand the sun, is part of the equipment of the pilgrim; perhaps hot-pink shoes are more appropriate stage props than water-proofed brogues. What matters is not how well-fitted for the journey a person is but how willing to engage in fierce and unequal combat. Don Quixote tilted at the world—tilted, a word I'm fond of. It conveys something oblique, from an angle, off kilter, catawampus. If I had to fight a windmill, whirlygigging incessantly, I don't see any other way to attack. But of course, I don't fight windmills, or giants, either, though to be perfectly honest I live on a street where I could fight windmills had I a mind to, because so many of my neighbors keep small, decorative windmills in their yards. Not in Great Britain, however—not on the cliffs of Cornwall or at the foot of Tintagel. And certainly tilting at windmills in the middle of a desert would appear even more ridiculous than arming myself against the windmills I jog by nearly every day of the year. Deserts by definition have no use for windmills.

However, Don Quixote, who has an answer for everything, would say I've missed the point, since he is fighting giants, not windmills. That's fine for the Don, but how many giants-cum-windmills or cum-anything have we seen recently? Is Tintagel a giant? Is a superhighway a giant? Are the circles of work-home-bed, work-home-bed, until we are bone-bored by the giants we face? Perhaps we have giants up ahead waiting for us, the giants of penance, or, worse, the giant of death.

Only recently have I begun to think of us pilgrims as the rogues of the road, ludicrously intense to the world of tourists; we're people making much of *not* much, and yet, there it is. How else am I to reconcile the differences between tourist and pilgrim that we have been struggling with? A tourist attends Stonehenge—or the desert—as a place to pass through, another notch on the camera, while we live there and fight our way to some understanding of why and what this desert or this circular bunch of rocks means. We look for patterns, we read the contexts, we strive to keep walking, no matter how many of our company pause at the Two Pigeons Inn, never to pick up the path again. Maybe the temptation to take the easy way, to give up the trip, is a giant in disguise.

But there seems more to being a pilgrim than seeing giants where others see windmills. It might be a matter of seeing ourselves, seeing ourselves clear. Why are we on the road? Because way back at the beginning we discovered that we couldn't reach our destination any other way, that there and back again wasn't good enough, because *there*, once we've found out about it, changed *here*, for good and all. So, no matter how ludicrous we know we look to those who are content with there and back, we've got to stick with there, giants or no giants.

Every pilgrim who ever put shoeleather onto hardpan has faced them. Sometimes giants have one large eye, dead center forehead; sometimes they look just like us, only bigger. Sometimes pilgrims plunk themselves on the bony ridge of brow, thinking they've found a nice boulder for a picnic, only to discover when the giant twitches his eye what a mistake they've made. Giants are natural enemies of the road, the quest, the adventure, the pilgrimage.

Giants can turn romance into a cheap horror show — the recently married couple who learns that one of them has cancer; the parents who discover drug paraphernalia in their daughter's room; the student who tries his best but nevertheless fails the chemistry final; the minority woman who works two or three jobs and still finds herself unable to pay her bills; the immigrant who wants to learn to read and write but finds a waiting list for the only class available because there isn't enough money to pay for more teachers, though the state will demean him with insignificant welfare checks. These are giants, though some people might call me foolish for thinking so. To that sentence, let me add those gold-hoarding, fire-breathing, gate-keeping *dragons*, dragons who don't let would-be pilgrims onto the path. Dragons and giants, the two fiercest foes of pilgrimage. Faced with such foes, I understand why some pilgrims never get farther than the Two Pigeons.

Of course, we could put this into New Testament imagery and talk of principalities and powers and rulers of darkness, the way St. Paul does. What would his audience have thought of giants and dragons, I wonder? But for this context, giants and dragons read better. We can call Milton to witness, or better yet, as guide that there are dragons on the wing, waiting to subvert us. Didn't he depict Satan leaving hell as a large, dragon-like creature? Foolish Satan, who thinks he looks as good as new, when we know he hasn't aged well since he fell from heaven: gold turned to tin, and tarnished, at that. Later he assumes the guise of a small dragon, that is, a serpent (as in the Garden of Eden), and then in hell after his triumph Satan and all his host become very large serpents, applause turned to hissing.

But Milton and Don Quixote? Milton who sent us on our way with weary steps and slow? How can he possibly guide us to understand the peculiar, picaresque particulars of pilgrimage? This enterprise is turning into a reader's white-elephant sale. Perhaps it is incongruous to include the loftiest poet and his loftiest poem as evidence that pilgrims face dragons and giants; however, there's more to Milton than high-flung syntax, and often when he's flinging his loftiest his tongue is deepest in his cheek.

Yet whether we choose Paul's metaphors or Milton's or those of Cervantes, we come to the same situation in the end: the trials of travel in a world that insists we tilt one way when every understanding we have of reality insists we tilt another. In that sense, all pilgrims become picaresque heroes who are more than foolish innocents loose on the world. And how do I define "picaresque heroes"? They are rogues and renegades, radical theologians and wild-eyed prophets, bent on providing that immigrant the resources of school and the minority woman meaningful work.

This adds yet another wrinkle to the business of being a pilgrim—transformers of the social order. Up till now pilgrims have almost seemed anti-social, separating themselves from the society they know is corrupt and corrupting. Isn't that part of the difference between the tourist and the pilgrim, the one taking his values from society in shopping-mall fashion, the other finding values in what society ridicules? For a pilgrim to hold that view of life can be difficult when faced with the lures of the easy road. Perhaps I am misreading the old tales when I claim that they help us see how deeply pilgrims travel into this world at the same time that they seem to be traveling out of this world by engaging the giants and dragons roaming the earth. This social/anti-social business is one more contrary on a road that has been bouldered with them. Paradoxes. I guess it is up and over once more.

But wait another minute. What began as a look at the juxtaposition of picaresque and pilgrimage has quickly become much more serious with all this talk of social corruption and social upheaval. Who twisted the signpost? I expected some light terrain, yet I seem to be facing the Scottish Highlands. Obviously, writers as well as readers bring certain expectations to a text; whoever shifted the signpost has upended my expectations entirely. Shouldn't a writer be able to control her own destiny, at least so far as words on a screen go? Shouldn't I be allowed to fulfill my expectations, just as everyone grants readers the same rights—to travel with the writer or to take the text and do with it what they will, even if it is merely to use the text to prop open a door?

After all the miles we've traveled I find this movement of the meaning unacceptable. I thought it was time for a bit of fun, as the Brits say, a comfortable amble into the picaresque particulars of being a pilgrim. I marked this chapter easy to moderate, intending to leave for another day and another chapter walks marked difficult. Experienced though we may be, even we need a day off from the knee-to-nose terrain. The cliffs of Tintagel create light-headedness, at least in me. Let's try to turn the signpost right side round.

Pictures come to mind, pictures that strike me as a picaresque version of the serious pilgrim paths we've been walking. Not the least is the picture of myself sitting in this dark chamber lighted only by my computer screen and the bright green words that appear in the wrong way in the wrong place, struggling to define what a picaro is. This Don Quixote lives his life on the path, though he also exists in the world most of us recognize as reality, the world of the normal social order. His creator wants us to recognize the multivalent nature of reality, that same reality we explored recently in recognizing our many simultaneous lives. It isn't a fact that we hold consciously, though it enables us to chase circles, yet be pilgrims all the same. A thoroughgoing picaro like the Don accepts his life in deserts, in mountains, and in shopping malls, all at once. The incongruities never deflect him from his task. What difference do a few contradictions or paradoxes make? Embrace them, the Don tells us. They are all part of the human condition of fighting giants and dragons where others see windmills, or conquering mountains where others see molehills.

But I am not the only picture I see, the only ridiculous figure on the horizon. I have companions who are equally ridiculous: a moorland of sheep and a dog. I find their picture appealing, in an innocent, irreverent way. Sheep are so stupid; there's no other way to put it. But in their stupidity lies such charm—in their eyes, the shape of their heads, the proportion of their bodies. I use the plural on purpose, for sheep come in genres just the way books and people do. And probably some genres are smarter than others, though the comparison is feeble, since none of them comes up to the mark of a dog: sheep and dogs, an ancient and noble combination.

My fascination with dogs and the sheep they herd has grown over the years, I suppose in itself ridiculous, since Americans have little opportunity to study sheep. We do, however, have some picture in mind when we hear the word *sheep*. Sheep and sheep stories have an ancient tradition in the literature of pilgrimage, so any account of pilgrims must include them.

Over the years my picture of sheep has changed. I once thought of them as rotund and woolly—round faces, round bodies, tightly curled and rounded wool; obviously I had never seen a shorn sheep—the typical down breed, the kind bred for food, not sweaters. Now I love to roll the names of various breeds off my tongue and handle the wool of each: Swaledale with its black and white angular face and long coat; the spotted Jacob, the kind the patriarch would have loved; the Shetland so well known for its soft fur; the Herdwick of the Lake district, with its blue-grey coat and long white face; the Wensleydale, whose fleece falls in loose ringlets, even down over its face; and the well-known Scottish blackface. These are only a few British breeds; Australia and New Zealand would have those and others, Middle Eastern countries still more, for each sheep is bred for a particular need— wool or food—for a particular terrain and temperature. The coarse coats on sheep that live in the wet, northern moorlands of Great Britain would not survive the heat and dryness of Israel.

But no matter how beautiful they appear sheep are still stupid: useful, entertaining, loveable, but stupid, at least according to all ancient traditions. I'm speaking here of domesticated sheep; sheep in the wild need as many stratagems of survival and some cunning as do other nonpredatory animals. Is it possible that we have bred stupidity into sheep? To compare ourselves to sheep, therefore, is less than flattering, for their behavior on the trail is erratic and baffling, as I've had opportunity to discover, for a pilgrim shares the path with all kinds of creatures—goats, cows, people, and sheep, especially sheep.

Their version of tilting at windmills is kaleidoscopic. They run from or to boulders, rocks, gorse, or cliff edge, for no apparent reason. Is the grazing better two feet to the left or right of them? Sheep are likely to let a passerby come close or to sheer off in fright. And if one does, they all do; sheep have the quintessential crowd mentality, always looking for the one right answer everyone should accept. When they choose to stand, they study a pilgrim with the intensity of a scientist, their jaws rotating methodically to masticate and tenderize their tough food. Staring back, we think that they must mean something by their intensity, until they barge off, bleating. Their voices are something to hear, each breed having its own vocal characteristics in addition to body and fleece type. Even males and females of a genre sound different, the females often bleating with the deepest resonance. They choir the pilgrim's path as no other creature can; a herd together is a formidable harmony. I wonder what sheep say to each other as they travel their well-marked paths; perhaps they encourage each other to keep on. But there's just as much evidence that they can't keep on; sheep carcasses are nearly as common as heather on moorland.

Don Quixote would tell us that all of life is example; so too with sheep, as others have said before us. We pilgrims wander like sheep, sometimes going astray, sometimes keeping on. We bleat incessantly at one another, telling each other the stories we need to create and sustain our society and so amuse ourselves as well as define ourselves, for stories do both, or ought to. They show us possibilities—possibilities for pilgrim living, possibilities for tourist living—they show us what might happen should we choose one possibility over the other. Amusement, though, should not be disdained for more serious matters. We can walk with our tongue in our cheek just as well as Milton—well, maybe not *that* well; epic poets are as scarce today as tourists are legion. We must walk with what we've got, which is, at the moment, Don Quixote. He's headed our way, just there, though you may not recognize him immediately.

Every sheep story must have a dog story embedded in it somewhere; it's part of the genre. The Old Testament king and shepherd, David, might not have needed a dog to nip the heels of his sheep, but most shepherds we've encountered not only come equipped with a stick, an equivalent of the shepherd's crook, but at least two black and white dogs to keep their herds headed correctly. Sheep that pasture on moorland wander blissfully ignorant of the sharp teeth of such dogs, assuming in their innocence that a day of reckoning will never come to them, though shearing time always does. Collecting the herds would be nearly impossible without sheepdogs. As anyone who has ever tuned in "All Creatures Great and Small" knows, watching these dogs is sheer delight. Small wonder sheep farmers are rightly proud of their animals and sheepdog trials are as common as county fairs in the summer. However, even here, in pastoral innocence, terror lies only a bark away, for dogs, like people, can go wrong. When a sheep dog does, the consequences can be devastating, as they were for Gabriel Oak in Thomas Hardy's *Far From the Madding Crowd*—his black and white dog methodically nipping the herd over the seacliff to death. The wild whispers of wickedness too great for dog to bear.

However, the picaro I have in mind has no such desperation in him, though he makes as strong an impression. He is an airedale who, if he ever worked, no longer does so. If you have pictured a beautifully groomed, short-coated animal, look again. This male airedale has not been sheared in some time, his coat matted and disreputable, hair hanging in his eyes. His gait, nothing more than a swaggering kind of slouch, adds to his persona, a dog fallen on hard times, a dog at odds with society. As he approaches, I recall the airedale who lives down our street, a trim, prosperous animal with every evidence of accepting the norms of society—or at least forced to by her people, though she gives some suggestion that if left to her own devices she would live as ragtag and antisocial an existence as does the male airedale who dogs our heels. Shammy's instincts run to mudpuddles and chasing ducks through stickers and brambles, especially after an expensive grooming.

On this particular day Allen and I had just begun to stretch our legs for a walk to a sheltered beachcove some miles east and north of us, our path taking us up and down sections of moorland, the mild Exmoor country, not so rugged as Yorkshire or so barren as Dartmoor. Our packs held raingear and a light lunch, as well as juice; if the day held fair, as it promised to, our burden would become heavier as the day wore on, for we would shed our outer layers, store them in our pack, and eventually reach our core clothes. Pilgrims sometimes spend more time dressing and undressing than walking.

We were lodged for the week at Holdstone Farm, a twelfth-century structure Jane and her husband had remodeled to accommodate them and their bed-and-breakfast guests. We were glad they had left intact the cobblestone courtyard, which led from the house to the barn. Holdstone was primarily a sheep farm; we had arrived at shearing time, almost the busiest time of the year for a sheep farmer (the other would be lambing). As we drove up the long drive from the road, the cacophony of barned sheep blocked out the sound of our engine.

Holdstone was an ideal location for us. Its back pastures overlooked the Devon coast, and it was just inside Exmoor, close enough for a short drive to the many interior walks, provided the fog stayed away. One of the pleasures of the path is hearing the tales of others, as I've said, and the tales Jane told us were no exception—stories of her husband's family, who had owned the farm for generations; descriptions of separating fleece by genre and bagging each one for market; and, of course, this being both moor country and horse country, tales of riders lost in the mist, horses up to their hocks in bog. "We've lost horses up there," Jane would intone in her broad Devon accent. When she said, about a horse she wanted to buy, "It would suit me down to ground," I wondered how firm that ground, and therefore the expression, really was.

Jane provided well for her guests, and since we were her only ones that week we got the best treatment— superb meals, tea, numerous tips and suggestions about where pilgrims might find the best ground for their feet. She didn't even mind that we were up before her for our daily jog; sheep farmers, unlike dairymen, we learned, didn't roll out of bed with the roosters. There must be some advantages to sheep, said Jane, after a day spent bagging coarse fleece from some far-north breeds.

"A-want no more of that lot," she told us. "And A've told m' husband that, as well." A wool merchant in explaining his stock of handspun, natural wool pointed out one that would wear for twenty years as a sweater, adding, "Then you can cut it up and use it for steel wool." Raw fleece can cut, as Jane's scratched hands showed.

At her suggestion we went in search of Heddon Mouth, an isolated spot on the sea. People have preferences in landscape, I've discovered. My husband leans toward mountains, natural since he grew up in them. But I long for the sea. I don't suppose I have been entirely content since I left the sea when I was fourteen, something only now, when I have written it, do I know. Most of us live so day-to-day with ourselves that we cannot see what ought to be obvious. The restlessness, the hunger, the frustrations become so habituated that we fail to recognize what drives us on pilgrimage, what pushes us for definition, discovery, what makes our life journey worthwhile. Not until I begin to recall my marrow-deep contentment as we greeted each section of coast, my reluctance to move, my longing to return, do I understand how seldom I feel that way. The angst of the woman in the paper returns to me, and I know, now, that I am also that woman, her angst a reflection of my own. I also feel even more the loss of Eden, the loss that initiated us into the petty tragedies that so much of life consists of. So I long for the sea.

I am doomed to a lifetime of restlessness, I realize, away from the sea, the sea an image of the relentlessness of life, the inevitability of dying, the knowledge most of us, myself especially, flee from. Yet paradoxically the purpose of pilgrimage is to prepare us to die, to make us ready, sinew and bone, for the last, most frightening, pilgrimage of all. And yet I long for the sea. It stretches and stretches and there seems no end to it; it disregards all of us, and of all God's creatures it has always seemed to me the most *itself*, the one that need not search for definition. Perhaps that is why Tintagel so captured me and why I envision my journey's end as a place much like it. I want no other Celestial City than one with salt spray in the air and white foam on the horizon. Knowing it awaits will make the final pilgrimage easier, if anything can.

Do all roads lead in one direction? Do all paths eventually wind their way just where we most long to be? While in Devon I couldn't seem to get enough of the sea, of looking at it, of walking its chilly edge, of tasting its brine. Whatever path we took we found ourselves headed seaward, a gift from my husband to wander with me since he does not have a magnet on which the sea pulls. Too immense, too big. Only ten years earlier he had first encountered the Atlantic off the coast of the Outer Banks of North Carolina. "You can't mean to *swim* in that, can you?" was the first question he could manage. No one could become that intimate with something that awesome. Only an inlander would worry about such a thing. Those who grow up side by side with the ocean have a more cavalier and at the same time a more respectful view of the sea.

It must be wonderful to live on an island where you are never far from shore, something I envy. Because it had been so long since the sea and I had talked about what counted in life, as soon as Jane told us about Heddon Mouth, where a river empties into the ocean, I knew I had found my path. Our walk began in rain at the farm, off over Heddon Down, past Hunter's Inn centered in the valley, and then into the woods to follow the river, to end in sun on the rocks of this isolated cove. The end for me the beginning of what I never wanted to end, my talk with the sea.

I have two versions of Heddon Mouth—at least two, as all pilgrims do who have encountered significant places on the path—the one in my mind, the other in my handwriting; although some pilgrims might have pictures, we were camera-less that year, so my pictures exist only behind my eyes.

I searched for the record I made of my visit to Holdstone and Heddon Mouth, certain that I had left no detail unmentioned—not the sheep, not the Airedale, not the sea. But my memory of my record is as faulty, perhaps, as my memory of the paths we took to the sea, not this one only, but many throughout the week, to different parts of the Devon coast, each different, each evocatively named, each significant. Why this seawash in a chapter on the picaresque I am not sure, cannot yet discover, though I see our slouching Airedale beside us; he too was searching for the sea. But he does not enter this section of the story, for he did not walk with us to Heddon Mouth, as my mind so clearly recalled for me, but which my journal belied. I find no dog, no sheepish pilgrim wagging beside us. His part comes later.

Even now, writing of Heddon Mouth and trying to fit the dog into that week-long, seaward search, I feel serenity conquer my anxieties. My neck relaxes, my shoulders loosen, my arms become limp, and all because the sea has taken me by surprise here in my sealess, sunless space. *Now*, not at Tintagel, though we had the sea in abundance there. Perhaps it was too remote in Cornwall, since I couldn't or wouldn't venture to the beach, a ridiculous figure, who couldn't conquer her fears to reach the real destination.

As I return to Heddon Mouth, I realize that it is not a memory I return to but a reenactment, which, in the reenacting becomes another experience entirely. Heddon Mouth is no past-tense experience; nor can I say it is present tense. Although some languages might have a syntax for this not-past—not-present existence, this mystical, mysterious, reliving, rereading, recreating of reality, English does not. All such experiences, then, become difficult to explain, since they go beyond the capability of our grammar.

If my experience at Heddon Mouth is one such event, surely another, and the most important, occurred two thousand years ago in a cramped, upper room. And so proclaim the Lord's death until he comes. The words connect the act and reenactment with a story. Proclaim. Tell. Narrate. Our lives are of such narration that we move between past, present, and future, just as the command to communion insists. All three tenses in one sentence, even in one verb: narrate. Or, in the words of the old gospel song, "Tell me the old, old story." What that song fails to say is the way the old, old story is rewritten daily in the lives of all pilgrims—or better still, how pilgrims' lives incarnate the story, even down to the dusty path whose purpose and destination inhere in the dust itself, and not just in the end of the road. Jesus said it best, "Do this in remembrance of me"; reenact my story.

But to reenact the story is to enact death. But how does death fit in with the picaresque in pilgrimage? If the picaresque is comedy, surely death is tragedy. In a comedy—unless it is very black indeed—no one dies. How can we laugh at death? Using medieval emblems as evidence, we see that there was a time when we did laugh. The grotesque, grimacing, jeering spaces of emblems and triptychs filled to overflowing with bodies and limbs floating in the artist's vision were created when the Black Plague was killing most of the population. Even without it and its recurrence over the next few hundred years, death was an ever-present reality. And yet they, not we, who spend billions of dollars a year to frustrate death, scorned it. Although the medieval emblems of death appear ridiculous to us today, if only because they translate Death into a literal character with a name and a personality, perhaps they hold more truth than we know, for isn't the upper room the beginning of the mirth? a kind of satire against Sin and Death, who think they have the final word as offspring of Satan?

And there lies the problem. We miss the satire. Or we forget it. Overlook it. Ignore it. How could we else? What do we know about perfection? Life? We know Sin and we know Death. We marry them, we birth them, we nurture them. Sin and Death travel with us everywhere, our constant companions, even those of us on this pilgrimage. When people were less enlightened, according to our notions of enlightenment, when people saw the world as physical and spiritual simultaneously, when metaphysics reigned, then they knew these truths: No matter where we walk, no matter how far or how fast, we cannot outstep Sin and Death. Their whispers infect the stories we tell and our reasons for telling them. They fill our ears with misreadings of the stories our fellow pilgrims tell us. They drive us to desperation, to flights of fear, to a willingness to risk anything, so they will leave us, leave us just for a day, or an hour, or a minute. I want to forget them. Yet everywhere I turn, with every path I walk, in every person I encounter, Sin and Death meet me. I cannot escape their stench. No matter how deeply I breathe the salt air of Heddon Mouth I smell decay underneath. The blue, beautiful sea yields up its dead with every wave, the sight of mortality unrelenting. And I remember Milton's Satan: "Which way I fly is hell, myself am hell." I, as an heir of Eve and Adam, share with Satan this reality.

I can refuse it, as I do this day, refuse to acknowledge what is always with me, the insecurity of never knowing when Sin and Death will have had enough of my pretending. Even at Heddon Mouth, even though I refuse to confess them as companions on this pilgrimage, even though I will not admit that they have been with me all along, from my first breath, from this first page, I find that it is not so. Why otherwise would I have written in the journal I began to carry that summer, "Now Allen is foolishly climbing an outcropping on his hands and knees." Why is this simply another Tintagel, another story I write in my head and on paper, another accident, another death? And so, what happened to my peace?

It is there. I can read it, here italicized, as well as remember it. *I sit, still, on a large rock and listen to the slam and crackle of the Atlantic as it sweeps across the pebbly beach— a sound unlike the ocean hitting sand.* I struggled to define the sound, finding that I was refusing Sin and Death even in so innocent a task. *What is the sound of water on pebbles like?* I had never heard it before. *Almost like parchment being crinkled—almost, but not quite, because that is close to paper being torn, which has an ugly connotation.* I had rejected the description as an image of destruction. *The sound occurs as the tide rolls back on itself toward the sea.*

What did I mean by that? It was a sound of receding, of undoing, of reversing, of those stones and the stone being rolled back. Sounds superimposing images on one another, Heddon Mouth, the Garden tomb, the final examination, success or failure hanging threadlike and tenuous. One slip, one mistake, one misreading, and all is failure, whether the task is climbing a cliff, taking a test, or rising from the dead. Yes, even that could have been a failure had all refused to believe that Jesus stood corporeal before them, as many of us have refused to believe since. "Readers, respond," God commands. "Infuse my act with meaning." If no one had believed, what then? Would there have been Resurrection? Even Jesus said that he could perform miracles—write a living text—*only* when readers participated in the meaning. The terrifying act of God is in giving us a choice. If only we had the form before us to neatly fill out, like too much of school, then it would be so easy. But there is no form; there is only choice—to commit or to refuse—whether in work, in school, in reading, in marriage, in parenthood, or in faith. And each commitment is an act reaching into the future, and so into uncertainty. Nothing so terrorizes us as commitment.

This is what I find between the lines of my journal about that day, the terror of not really knowing, the reason I talked to the sea. Or I thought I did, though I find nothing explicitly recorded, no questions, no answers, no such stories as Anne Morrow Lindbergh found when she talked to the ocean. Her record in *Gift from the Sea* goes beyond mine, her pilgrimage more certain, more focused. I was out of practice, and the beach at Heddon Mouth was only the first of my talks, or should I say my exchange, with the sea. A saltwater transfusion for my soul's health. Its living energy with the underlying odor of death first cauterizing my wounds, then its brine washing my wounds clean, and its breezes suturing them.

As I have so many times before, I stumbled forward without a clear reason as to why I needed to reach this place; nor could I control what happened. My part was to put myself in the way of healing, once and for all, I assumed. Yet it is in the nature of pilgrims to need healing over and over again; once for all is less realistic than once upon a time. Each encounter with briars, or each fresh reminder that Death still whispers, requires another cauterizing and cleansing. We walk like spirals and Slinky toys, recursively, geometrically, paradoxically.

When we need healing, though, we don't always

have the sea close to hand. Sometimes healing comes through some form of the comic: burlesque, mock-epic, satire, or the picaresque; and here I find my path back to the main trail, for our hero, Don Quixote, seems so sea-breeze well in his unself-conscious walk. Why am I drawn to the Don when clowns repulse me? I think I now understand. Most clowns never lose the self-consciousness that they are ridiculous; they intend to call attention to themselves, thus their shrieking color and costume, which say, "Look at Me! See Me make you laugh!" And I won't. The Don, on the other hand, says, "Look at that. There lies danger. Adventure. Life to conquer. Beauty to explore. Things to learn." He never, ever, says, "Look at *me*," for he is not the center of the pilgrimage. Rather, he asks for companionship and commitment to walk side by side up the road, studying the horizon, considering the destination, anticipating the next bend and the Inn with smoke coming from the chimney and the smell of food coming from the door. We don't know what will come, but we know with whom we will share the journey and the stories of the journey.

The ocean says the same; no one can, for long, consider the sea without understanding that she or he is not the center of the path. If the Don is ridiculous, it's all part of the pilgrimage, his story, and he never stops to look in the lake to see for himself why others think he is so amusing. He, like the sea, is simply himself, his own definition.

I doubt that I can ever fully achieve the stature of the picaro; my self-consciousness counters my every attempt. Self-consciousness is a face-saving term for self-centeredness, for ego. To let go of myself, which I recognize as a necessary condition for pilgrimage, so frightens me that I hold on to myself in spite of my resolve not to. I am a trapeze artist who cannot let go out of fear that my partner will not reach me before I fall, and there is no net beneath me.

However, it isn't only the fear of losing myself that at times prevents me from full pilgrimage; it is also a paucity of models. Not models in books or stories, as necessary as they are, but models who live and breathe with me. Right now I can only think of one model: the Airedale who picked us up on our way to Sillery Beach some seven miles or so beyond Heddon Mouth, well down the Devon Coast. A pilgrim for a day, he surprised and entertained us. I know that I can never approach his insouciance.

In Great Britain, dogs have status, as great a class structure among them as there is among their owners, though accent does not reveal it. If that is so, this Airedale, let's call him Ralph, would be lower than Cockney, lower than Birmingham, though he obviously hadn't a care about Society, as we soon discovered. He was no Etonian.

We were limbering our legs for a long day when we passed him on the road. He eyed us as we approached, sizing us up the way we'd seen walkers do, wondering whether we were up to his company. Although he may not have cared about Society, that didn't mean he had no standards. To give us his presence, he wanted to know that we saw reality from his perspective. No point in pilgrims fighting all day.

We had passed him and turned toward Heddon Down when he joined us. Since footpaths in the UK cross private land, we assumed that he would stay with us until we left his territory and moved to another's. In the meantime we would enjoy his recursive approach to pilgrimage, for like all dogs Ralph found our pace a little slow for his liking. He rushed ahead, circled around, spooked a few rabbits, circled back, snuffled at our heels, and then, when he saw that his advice to keep pace would not be heeded, once more ran ahead. His antics made us laugh. Every breeze-swept bush, every shadow, became for Ralph giants and dragons to meet in fierce and mortal combat. We soon understood his relationship to us—that of knight errant, protector. In coming along he had not flattered us but taken pity on us. The knowledge was humbling.

Although the first several miles we speculated when and where he would turn back, our talk changed to wondering whether he would stay with us throughout the day. Soon we became accustomed to his presence. There is a certain body language among companions that distinguishes us from those who by happenstance are in close proximity to one another, such as people leaving a theater or concert hall together. Sometimes I try to determine who is with whom. The same body language existed with Ralph. He told people that he belonged to us, which occasionally put us in an awkward position, though, as I said, such societal considerations bored Ralph.

All dogs on footpaths were supposed to be leashed, which, obviously, Ralph wasn't. Walkers with dogs who violated that rule had annoyed us, and here through no intention of our own we were doing the same. Ralph was our companion, yet he wasn't ours. Walkers who glared at us and such a disreputable companion didn't slow down to hear the story; either they pitied us, disliked us, or thought us irresponsible owners to allow a dog to appear as he did. Those were the ones without dogs themselves.

The walkers we came to dread were those with dogs, especially well-groomed and obviously pampered creatures. Something about Ralph's swagger told us and them how disgusting he found them. He barely deigned to give them a sniff. Of course, these were always the dogs on leash. Owners had a distinctive way of conveying their contempt for us by a snap of their wrist, as they pulled back their animal. "Is this your dog?" was the inevitable question. We heard it so often that we began to apologize and explain almost before the walkers were within hearing; often they passed our words without a nod. Ralph would turn and cock a reassuring ear at us. Why should we give a thought to such shallow thinkers, when he didn't? They were aligned with the Other.

Ralph certainly had a clear sense of Right and Wrong and where the Other was to be found. It wasn't quite *our* sense, but then picaros pay no attention to such failure of vision. Ralph was also a chauvinist. There was no denying this blindspot. Although he pitied and protected both Allen and me, he allowed Allen some greater freedom because of their shared maleness. I, as a female, stood more in need of aid than my male companion. So, when we made a rest stop in the Valley, Ralph accompanied me to the door and stood guard until I exited. "I think he likes you," Allen said. "At any rate, he's adopted you." I must have looked skeptical or disgruntled, as if we had returned to Tudor England where all females were ruled by some male—father, husband, brother: Dog. Ralph, I decided, had decidedly too high an opinion of himself.

However, he didn't seem to have any intentions of taking off without us. As we turned upcountry toward Sillery Beach, a decision he approved, he took the role of scout. He scouted so far in advance that we thought we had seen the last of him that day; but each foray forward always ended in his return. We came to accept his hit-and-miss presence, so that when we met an Airedale-loving couple we nearly preened when they fussed over Ralph, as if we had in any way shaped his fix on himself and the world. This time we only reluctantly admitted he was none of ours, though, as the gentleman pointed out, he seemed like ours.

The walk to Sillery Beach wound around and around the seacliffs, not as narrow a path as some we had walked but not always wide enough for three abreast, certainly not if we met walkers headed where we had come from. On those occasions, and because the path offered a long view of what was ahead, we could watch Ralph's surges and returns and gauge our forward progress by his. When it came to a choice of which fork to take, Ralph knew the right one, almost as if he could read as well as we the footpath signs and understood our destination. He would not be lost, no matter how we dawdled.

When we came down off the path to the paved road that led toward the beach, we entered the high-rent district, Boardwalk and Park Place. Two sweaty walkers and a harum-scarum dog were as out of place here as fleas in the Queen's pajamas. Newport or the Hamptons, sections of the private gold coast of New Jersey, these came to mind as we followed the serpentine road to the shore; and in this country Sillery Beach would have been signposted private, the American aristocracy of wealth privileging itself and protecting itself against the middle-class rabble of which we were so obviously members. Well, given the fellowship of Ralph, maybe even worse than middle class—intellectual leftwingers, picaros. I was even more certain of it when we passed a Victorian Inn overlooking the beach, the vacation spot of the leisured British class and, to our regret, the not-quite-Newport but well-to-do Americans we encountered on the final, downward slope. At least they were heading up.

How they knew we were Americans, particularly since we were dogged that day, I cannot remember— knew when the Brits we encountered never did. After the ritual exchange of "Where are you from," "How long have you been here," and "When do you return," with the traditional chorus of "What have you done"—freely interpreted, what have you finished, exploited, used up, consumed, the consummate question of the tourist—we moved on, trying to avoid Ralph's accusing eyes: I *can't* have hooked myself up with two of *them*. Our fellow citizens were, of course, staying at the inn; the possibility of sharing a bath in a bed and breakfast was not accommodating enough.

My reading of the road proved somewhat accurate, as we passed a private drive, another resort hotel, and encountered two of the most moneyed, powerful, and privileged dogs I can think of (if this is beginning to sound ideological lay the blame to Ralph and his interpretation of Don Quixote; when I think about the picaresque I can't avoid walking into that region): a poodle and a Russian wolfhound. I can't think why they come into the story together, but there it is. Or rather, there they were, with Ralph serving as Falstaff to the newly crowned Prince Hal, now Henry V: Bow, please. Neither Falstaff nor Ralph were prepared to do so.

This is a tale of extremes: ornery Airedales, petted poodles, and haughty wolfhounds. I'm certain that wolfhounds bear the aristocratic stamp. Why else would advertisers pair them with willowy women and luxury cars foregrounded in space only the modern nobility could afford? Now that I'm advertising bound I can't recall ever seeing Russian wolfhounds in single units. Don't they always come in pairs when they're paired with willowy women who always come paired with luxury cars? Perhaps those dogs can only function when coupled.

Now I'm straining to see the dogs at Sillery Beach, and the more I look the more certain I become that, though the poodle was the proud owner of an elderly gentlewoman, the wolfhound was really a pair of wolf-hounds attached to a man and a woman. I am sitting on a rock on the beach, facing seaward with Ralph at my feet, where, after a brief paw-dipping excursion to test the waters, he remained, until voices startled us and I looked over my left shoulder to face the aristocracy.

I could tell Ralph did not approve of the intrusion, and to tell the truth, neither did I. Having the sea so seldom by my side made me jealous of sharing it with anyone. Ralph and I exchanged a brief look, with Ralph explaining that he would try his best to rid us of these sullied bourgeousie. I know he said *sullied*. They didn't look it to me. Ralph was the one who looked sullied— well, downright dirty. But trying to look at it from Ralph's sociological perspective I suppose *sullied* fit the four of them. He as much as said that here were the British equivalents of those awkward American consumers we had encountered earlier, the kind who were unkind to the land, who saw the sea and this rocky coast as a private theater for their entertainment and use. As something Other, not as something of which they were intimately a part.

Ralph was making a theological statement, I realize now. The four had no notion of themselves as creatures of a Creator who also created the space they consumed. No wonder Ralph tilted his way toward them. Here were giants and dragons to be dispatched, and he said as much.

The wolfhounds were visibly offended; that much was clear to me in the quiver of their noble noses and shuddering shoulders. The vibrations moved from the leash to the hands that held them. Ralph had done it this time. This was, after all, a public beach, regardless of someone's theological or sociological convictions. Like all picaros, Ralph tended to forget that.

Since I was too far away to hear the conversation, I can't report what he said and, though I could make something up, I'm sure Ralph would prefer that I be as accurate, or should I say as truthful, as possible. Nor was he any more forthcoming about this than he had been about his origins; it was enough to allow me to infer certain things about him, a kind of dog test of my intelligence and perceptivity. I can report that he returned to my rock with more than his usual swagger of accomplishment, and indeed the wolfhounds soon took their owners back up the path that led to and from the beach. With no further disturbances, I was able to concentrate on recording my impressions of the beach, after we finished our lunch of cheese sandwich and orange juice. While I wrote and Allen explored, Ralph remained at my feet, a strange experience for someone who is not by nature fond of dogs, a sentiment my cats share. But Airedales, this one in particular, began to win me over.

I tried Ralph's patience as we sat on the beach; clearly, he thought a beach is a beach is a beach. I couldn't argue that all beaches share certain characteristics in order to deserve the name beach—water, shore; I find the list stops there. I was going to write, "rock," but not all

beaches are rocky; I was going to write, "sand," but some
beaches aren't sandy. Nor could I write "blue" water or
"seagreen" water, for there are as many colors of water as
there are beaches. The water near the northernmost
beaches of Lake Michigan, for example, though it cannot
rival the ocean since it lacks salt spray, changes from a
violet close to shore to teal away from the shore. I could
not even say that all beaches share whitecaps or waves,
because these depend on the wind, for one thing, and so
vary with the weather.

Not even seaweed is a constant, and seaweed finds
its way from water to shore. It even once found its way
onto our front stoop after a particularly violent storm the
summer we lived in Niantic, Connecticut, across the street
from the beach. Was that the last time I was entirely
content? Or will I get skin cancer because I rushed
through my three meals to return like the ebb and flow of
the tides themselves to the beach? Bedtime always came
too soon; morning couldn't come soon enough; and
laundry was no problem for my mother when all we wore
were bathing suits. I welcomed the seaweed on our stoop,
just as I welcomed the seawater that flooded the streets.
Since I had paid the ocean so many visits, I felt it only
right that it reciprocate; but my mother had learned her
lesson: no more riding through hurricane eyes. I couldn't
even peak through the hurricane shutters all houses in
Connecticut bore to watch the progress the storms made.
Only adults, I supposed, were privileged to ride the
center, as my mother had.

But Ralph had no such memories to draw on, no
such connections with the puppy he had been, while I
relived as many connections with the ocean as I could
each time I plunked myself rockward. I wouldn't have

chosen any other place to be a pilgrim than this coastal
path. The sight of the changeling ocean made me a willing
journeyman, but there's more desert than ocean in most
pilgrim paths, and pilgrims by definition are movers, so
we couldn't stay indefinitely on Sillery Beach, which itself
refused us permission. High tide was very high. So we
turned to retrace our steps.

Normally we preferred a path that returned us a
different way than we had come, but in a beach pilgrimage there is no roundtrip possible, which we learned to
appreciate, because the returning path never looked the
same, though logically it should. Or at least, I thought so.
Ralph, whose story this is, as I seem to be forgetting by
remembering seaweed on front stoops, took a different
view, one of bored forbearance. Naturally, a picaro must
get back once he's got where he was going and faced the
dragons down—but he doesn't need to dawdle doing so.
So far as Ralph was concerned, we were dawdling. I'm
certain that was the source of his whimpering, whining
concern when, some time later, I stopped at an inn to
inquire about tea. He began when I walked through the
door and didn't stop until I came out a few minutes later.
At the time, we thought he was distressed by my absence,
afraid for my safety, upset that I had abandoned him. My
husband, who attempted to soothe him, insists still that
Ralph was distraught over my brief absence; he reads the
incident differently than I.

But those are romantic notions unbecoming a picaro.
Ralph couldn't have been so upset; no, he was merely
testy that I had dared pause when the adventure was not
over. It disrupted the fittingness, the rhythm of the story,
like a preacher who doesn't know when he's come to the
end and so keeps on and keeps on when his congregation

has exited his discourse. I don't know why Ralph put up with such a breach of decorum; digressions are all well and good, he told me, but enough is enough. So halfway home, perhaps fearing another such sidetrip, he took off. We never saw him again, though we passed the farm-house numerous times where we had first met him.

Companions

. . . .

I missed Pentecost this year, how I can't recall, but it must have slipped by me when I retreated north in June from a Sunday to a Sunday, one of which was probably Pentecost. This disturbs me, because it disrupts my rhythm and the rhythm of this pilgrimage. Beginning in Advent and moving properly through Christmas, Lent, and Easter, I had planned on Pentecost. Not that most of us are too aware of it as a holiday, or, to go back to the original meaning of that word, a holy day. Christmas and Easter, those are the big ones. Meaningless, however, without Pentecost, when tongues of fire and winds fiercer than hurricane force swept the disciples into direct political and religious conflict with Jerusalem and Rome, until politics and religion came together, probably to the detriment of them both. Pentecost also turns tourists into pilgrims.

Holy days are scarce—as scarce as holy places—though we've got holidays aplenty. Such a strange pilgrimage that word *holiday* has made, paralleling the pilgrimage of our society. Words, as writer Lewis Thomas reminds me, have a history. Another Lewis, C. S., in his book *Studies in Words*, also tells me that in words we can read the history of our culture. I find that here as in so much else pilgrims have traveled before me. I stop to find the essay where the two Lewises come together, written by Thomas, who quotes the other one, the skeptic turned Christian. Not here, in the several bookcases by my computer. It must be at school in my office there. I'll just forget it.

But I can't. I want that essay, feel the need of it to get me back to Pentecost, so I climb the stairs and in climbing the stairs I move from one climate to another. I have missed Pentecost, and it is hot up there, hot and humid, while down here where I write the air is cool and dry. Yesterday it reached 95, with the wind blowing everything in sight forty-miles-an-hour dry. My laundry on the line took an hour. Lying in my hammock and thinking I had missed the tongues of fire I did not realize how Pentecost-like the day, until now when I move from one world just a few stairs up to another.

The book wasn't in that world, either. It must be at school. And I realize again how fragmented my life is with three offices, one seven miles from here. As I look for the little book I have in mind I notice others that I had not thought of for years—*Johnny Tremain* and *The Soul of the New Machine*, a book called *Third Helpings* by Calvin Trillin, which I've never read. My husband bought it. I know because I don't find my name on the flyleaf, nor the date. I label my books with both, as my mother and grandmother before me did. When I buy used books, I look for those marks of ownership and recall what books I was marking while a Bill Johnson with his spiky, uneven hand was doing the same for a Joan Didion.

I want to pause and consider each of these books. Although they aren't the ones I want and need, perhaps they will serve, instead, for I am uncertain of what connections I seek; my only certainty is that I need connections, feeling their lack like bones empty of marrow. So as I reach out to pull off the shelf *The Language Gap*, or Isak Dinesen, I notice a narrow, blue spine. Lewis Thomas. Not the one I want, I discover, leafing quickly through the volume, nodding in remembrance at some essays, puzzled by others. One catches my attention: "Why Montaigne Is Not a Bore."

I'm interested in Montaigne these days, extremely interested. His name keeps crossing my path. Where had I read it recently? In a footnote to a line in *The Duchess of Malfi*, an early seventeenth-century revenge tragedy, where everyone dies by the end of the play. In the margin I had written two months ago, "use in pilgrimage book." I haven't, yet, but I will when the path turns just the right way. We'll die, too, at the end.

Where else have I found Montaigne? In the introduction to the 1989 volume of *Best Essays*. The general editor tells me Montaigne is back in the voice and in the words of dozens of modern essayists, who find their fatherhood in him. I understand that. And in my local used bookstore on the hunt for Aristotle I discover Montaigne. Although tempted, I leave him there for another pilgrim not so fastidious about reading the first English translation, the one Lewis Thomas mentions. He finds Florio tough going but worth the effort.

I even hesitate to mention Montaigne, for he and I have yet to become intimates. Thomas, however, pulls me forward. I begin to read what I have no recollection of reading, this essay on Montaigne, though I know I read it; I have this sense of guilt if I skip any part of a book, as if I have insulted the writer, somehow played bad faith, failed to hold up my end of the bargain.

Hear snatches—"It is the easiest of conversations

with a very old friend," says Thomas. "By the way," writes Montaigne, and Thomas writes that we're off on yet another story of himself. I learn that Montaigne is a moralist, a humorist, a man intent on understanding himself in order to understand what it means to be a human being. But we're inconsistent, inconstant, contradictory. We're too many people all at once on too many journeys that we just can't seem to harmonize, too seduced by the side track, fortunate for us, since the side track is often the right track.

Montaigne, writes Thomas, sees us as a "patchwork, so shapeless and diverse in composition that each bit, each moment, plays its own game." I find no better evidence for this than in our shift from holy days to holidays. I don't know about you, but holy days have a different voice about them than holidays, as different as, say, the slow, sonorous, and never-boring voice of Montaigne trying to figure himself out, a job he knows is fated to fail but one he thinks worth the meddle, from the voice of the anonymous wire-service report in the daily newspaper. A person doesn't fritter away a holy day. A sandy romp with a Frisbee seems quite in keeping with a summer holiday, but hardly appropriate for a holy day, Pentecost or any other. That "i" in holiday makes all the difference.

We like inconsequential play, and we need it, surely, but we also need holy days. Or maybe we need holy days that are part pomp and part play, as they were when the word retained its "y." But such play as was had then would hardly be considered so today. How many of us would turn out on Christmas or All Saints' Day for a traveling morality play? Since I don't know what I was doing on Pentecost, I can't classify my behavior as either pomp or play, though I suspect I was working, worst of all—working when I should have been receiving and giving.

So I have missed Pentecost and in missing it I have somehow lost my way and must trust that I can stumble back to the path I am meant to travel. All of the path should have been leading to Pentecost, which should then have provided an internal signpost for further walking, as it did for the disciples, who, once Pentecost had a grip on them, wore out more sandals than most of us do.

Strange behavior, that's what Pentecost wrought. Strange, dizzy, drunken behavior. If any group of people looked to outsiders more like a collection of Don Quixotes tilting at windmills, I can't imagine who it might be. Indeed, some observers thought the Pentecost crowd was drunk, not an auspicious beginning for the lifetime pilgrimage each was to start as a result of the heat and wind of the day. But our enterprise could hardly have begun better. It doesn't pay to look like the next guy when you're going against the likes of Jerusalemites and Romans.

Yet something happened to us along the way. The Church, with the mind of the modern marketer, turned pagan holidays into holy days, which we then managed to turn back into holidays, so that the only sacred thing about our calendar is the reverence we have for time off— and Sundays' numerals in red ink. Holiday carries us away from reality, not deeper into it, which, it seems to me, was the intent of holy days. The Church turned shopping mall for the consumer in us. And woe to those who, like Don Quixote, dare to show us what we refuse to see. The only way to deal with such people is to turn them into cartoon creatures or allow them an existence at the margins of society—modern-day lepers. Yet the more I read about picaros, dangerous, subversive actors, the more I realize how serious-minded they are; their adventures have life-and-death consequences. If viewed from its history, *picaro* means vagabond, tramp, someone outside, an Other—someone just like Jesus, I now realize.

I have condemned those who view picaros as charming, amusing innocents, society's fools, but the condemnation turns on myself, a renegade torpedo seeking a target. It takes courage to willingly appear the fool, a courage I don't have, for I would go to almost any lengths not to appear so. The persona I want to project to the world is that of a competent, confident, informed, realistic, and clear-sighted actor in this world's affairs. I cringe at the thought that I might stumble on the stairs, stumble in front of even a few people. It makes the life of a pilgrim difficult for me; no, it makes it nearly impossible. A pilgrim can't write a flawless script and say her lines without flubbing, for a pilgrim despite all the movement on stage isn't in charge, isn't the director. For someone who likes being in charge, and I do, that's the hardest lesson, and the most important lesson, pilgrimage has to teach. A picaro, on the other hand, takes naturally to appearing the fool. Although I want to accept this, I rebel, here, in the late innings of pilgrimage, at accepting the rules.

But there's more to my rebellion than a fear of embarrassment. I also have to confess that unlike Ralph, unlike Don Quixote, unlike the disciples, I don't want to find my fellow pilgrims and exchangers of stories in a society made up of the ridiculous, the poor, the disenfranchised, the discarded. I'm not comfortable with goatherds or lepers disfigured by disease. St. James talks about *me*, a respecter of persons, no matter how I try to fight that tendency. Sometimes the whispers work so loud in my ear that they drown out the stories I ought to hear, whispers that tempt me to think better of myself than I ought, whispers that tell me that this crowd I've set off with isn't really my crowd, that I'm only along for the walk.

In distancing myself in this way I deny the very community I have been so insistent we pilgrims need. These whispers of one-upmanship, of martyrdom, and of pride—St. Paul heard them too. I've always wondered if he knew what he was writing and revealing when he claimed to be the "chiefest of sinners"—one-upmanship with a vengeance. No matter what he claimed for himself it always carried the superlative—that *-est* inflection in English. Which then makes me fear what I've revealed or what you have read between my lines. There it is—that fear of foolishness, of appearing the ridiculous Don Quixote, of others not seeing the giants I see or the dragons I face. Or seeing, and not caring. It's enough at times to make me want to forsake language entirely, both spoken and written, which is as much as to say to forsake the human condition and the pilgrim road. If I never say anything, then I can never appear stupid and foolish. More than once have I set out for a meeting or a party committed to keeping my mouth shut, only to berate myself later for failing, yet again, to do so.

These confessions show how unprepared I am to be a pilgrim, as it shows, again, how far we—or at least I—have come since holy days turned into holidays. It is easy to accept the empty chatter of the holiday party—"nice to finally put a face to a name," phrases we repeat over and over, to the same people, from occasion to occasion, knowing we don't really want connections. We merely want the appearance of connections, a sort of pseudo-commitment, all the time shouting with our body language, "Don't get too close," words we can't speak. We unwillingly listen to people trying to reveal their story to us, trying to connect themselves to us, asking us to connect ourselves to them, such rude or inappropriate talk. We run from people whose eyes reveal a hunger for acceptance and support; they want more than we can give, and they know it. I know it, when I shop for listeners.

The human condition: A burden to tell our story, which means that we must hunger for the story of all kinds of other people; that is what a life journey is all about. Yet we have stepped onto a path for which we are not prepared, because our culture denies us such preparation. If we want to go, then we simply must walk off one day, leaving behind the shopping-cart chatter. Yet no one, in the days when pilgrims were pilgrims in earnest, would begin a pilgrimage without long, careful planning and lots of talk. The culture of the old tales provided for the pilgrim and asked for—demanded—his prayers along the way. The culture of the old tales knew the value of ritual.

A pilgrimage might have been holy but it was no holiday, in late twentieth-century terms. Many pilgrims died before reaching their destination, because dangers were real, the hardships great, far greater than for those Puritans who pilgrimaged to the New Land. And the trips lasted longer, two or three years, at least. A pilgrim did not sneak off: rather, a great village leave-taking, replete with holy ceremony and devotion, the culmination of months and months of preparation. So far have we come when I can write that inherent to pilgrimage is a *lack* of preparation. It's almost as if I resist ritual, refuse to acknowledge my need for it, a child of my culture. In sneaking off I can avoid the public spectacle of fool and failure.

There may be another reason, however, to avoid the ballyhoo at the beginning: Our path lies easy before us. We need not worry about papal licenses or preparing our will. We don't have to warn our creditors we won't be around for some years; we pay up or we pay as we go, thanks to international mail and FAX machines. Nor do we carry food and cooking utensils, though we might, indeed we ought, to carry a book or two to guide us on our way. Montaigne, perhaps? An ordnance survey map? And no matter who we join, no matter how seldom we would otherwise seek such company, when we become pilgrims we assert our equality. If we can't accept this and the other risks involved in pilgrimage, then we had better get out of the way of those who can. This I say to myself, a chant of my pilgrim path, my dragon that fires before me.

Well, I know I will fail; that too is something I must learn to accept, just as Peter did, just as John. Peter certainly flubbed his first chance at fighting his dragons and giants. Just like Frodo, who walked all the way to the Mount of Doom and then could not give up the ring, so Peter couldn't say, "I knew him, I walked with him, I was part of his pilgrim band"—his mount of doom. The language of the New Testament makes it clear how much easier he and the other disciples found counting fish than feeding sheep, if only because of the social and economic implications of those acts.

We're fond of giving up responsibility, or at least I am, which is another confession I must make and perhaps in making it I find another reason why pilgrimage is so hard and yet so essential. It's too convenient for me to place the responsibility for my behavior onto someone else, anyone else, even God, than put it where it belongs. When I do that to myself, or to others, I deny that I am human, something that not even God does. He insists that we are responsible for our actions; he makes no excuses for us. As the book of Genesis reveals, and Milton so eloquently restates, God insisted that our progenitors 'fess up. We can't hide. I sin, without provocation much of the time, though I find myself excusing my sin as a response to another's behavior: response not responsibility; that is the word I choose, and though they share the same root they do not share the same meaning. The longer I walk as a pilgrim the more I learn things about myself that I would rather keep hidden, hidden from others as well as from myself: my fears, my sins, my failures. But pilgrims can't travel long with their pretensions and personas intact. Nor can they walk for long without realizing the need for penance, which, like Pentecost, is something we don't talk about much any more.

It's strange how modern psychology has tried to recover what the Reformation removed, this need to pay what we owe—not that we can, though undoubtedly there were some who believed literally that penance bought them a one-way ticket to eternity. But penance as a physical act that is also metaphorical, representing a reality beyond our senses, seems to serve a psychological need. I need to make good the wrong I've done, not— merely—be forgiven. Otherwise, we live with unfinished business.

Pilgrimage is a pathway of penance, as well as a pathway toward penance. If I fit James's mold for a respecter of persons, then what better penance than to learn that each human being carries the weight of glory. If I would rather escape responsibility, what better penance than to walk knowing I must fulfill my part so that others can fulfill theirs. If I take too much responsibility on myself, then what better penance than to learn the reciprocity of interdependence. Yet, at the same time, in the tension points of the pilgrim life, I know that I am not actually creating the circumstances for my forgiveness nor receiving it by what I do. But I am, certainly, putting myself in the way by which I can receive or even see that forgiveness walks with me. Walks with me and whispers to me just as surely as does the Sin and Death I try to flee. In doing so, I declare myself, accept myself, human—a *mensch*, in Jewish terms.

But what am I really repenting? Aren't I repenting the presence of Death, the presence I fear as mortally as nothing else? Escape. I long for escape. Sin and Death haunt me and attack me when I am most secure in life. The specter of Death, the emblems of it: worm-eaten hags, skulls leering hungrily from the grave, frightening when we cannot tell a grin from a grimace. Perhaps I have read too many deathplays, looked at too many etchings of death personified, chewing up life faster than a colony of termites feed on fresh wood, orgiastic consumption. Once we lived under the threat of the Black Plague; today, I've read, we live under the threat of Nuclear Holocaust, the death angst of our late century. But that doesn't touch me, a holocaust that is too impersonal, too removed. That isn't the Death that grabs at my hand or shoulders, gripping me so hard as to make my teeth shake and saying Look. Look there. That's you in that coffin. Those worms are feeding on you—and no one knows, no one cares.

If only I could anticipate it, I might be able to stiffen

my resolve not to look. But I can't. Watching Franco
Zeffirelli's *Romeo and Juliet* it happens. Suddenly. I glance
away from the screen and with a shock I see a coffin, my
body lowered into it, and watch its disintegration into
dust, far faster than it will really happen. This has
occurred before, this shock of recognition, though not in
this context—walking down a city street and catching a
reflection in a store window. Then I know. That is my
face.

But in my death scene I never see my face, and I
wonder why. Would I recognize it as my own? Or would
it look like a distant cousin, someone whose face bears
only the vaguest stamp of the person I was. Or will it
show, finally, what life made of me, or I of it? No. No
life—no face. Not really. So I understand the reason for
death masks, to hide a face that no longer defines, as a
face is supposed to. Better a stylized, obviously unrepre-
sentational mask than a face that ought to be what it is
not. I know my face in the store window, I know it in the
mirror, I do not know it in death—cannot even imagine
what I will look like then, if "I" is even appropriate. Give
me a death mask, a disguise, a ritual, a protection; let no
one see what is no longer to be seen. But no matter how I
try to forget, to hide, to pretend, I see my coffined body,
my future.

Death. Denial. Hatred. All present in an instant of
revulsion, a vision that takes far less time to watch than to
tell. It cannot be, I whisper to myself over and over; it
cannot be that I and those I know will suffer this. It cannot
be that microbes are working their way toward my
grandmother, who died finally, willingly, during the
writing of this book, while I still find refusal of her death
easier than acceptance.

How much cleaner, less ugly, to write *microbes* or *spores*, than *maggots*. Those words of science ring with silver-metal and white-wall hygiene; maggots stink, they live in filth, they thrive in decay, a word, I have read recently, that in all cultures carries a stigma; we cannot scour the word clean. I do not want decay for my grandmother. I cannot accept this for myself. I don't deserve it, I say; despite my sins I don't deserve it: No one does.

And yet all I know, intellectually, tells me I should not feel myself while still alive being eaten away by death, every breath bringing me closer to breathlessness. Even Pentecost, that life-breathing holy day that I missed this year, even Pentecost signals death, and not least because it came as the result of the tomb; but also because some only observe drunks and fools, not Spirit-soaked picaros about to begin the most demanding pilgrimage of their lives. And those observers, who see windmills instead of dragons and giants, will die without knowing the three-day reversal from maggots and decay.

For that is part of Pentecost, the reversal of the picture, action undone, or redone better than before. While pilgrimage may present death undisinfected, it also presents a destination beyond death, beyond the maggots, beyond decay. On the other side. Death becomes a conduit through which the rush of the Holy Spirit pours and pushes us into the reservoir of life. If only I could see that, instead of my own entombing.

I have tried, certainly, as we all have, with occasional success, when joy as wide as the fear is deep holds me tight. Is this what pushed such a man as Johannes Brahms to write his second symphony, this straining to see beyond the maggots and the decay, when he felt madness threatening to engulf him? Anton Bruckner too, haunted by such visions, was driven to doubt and despair of everything, including the astonishing majesty of his own music. Trapped, he rewrote and rewrote his scores, attempting to overcome the prison of imperfection—of death—that refused birth to the music he heard and could not get to come right on paper. Did he scribble music to himself in the margins, notes from the grave? Did he feel his life confined to those margins, never able to move into the center of the page? When I think of the dark vision of so many people who bequeathed us a beauty that helps us surmount the despair of death, at least for an hour or two, I wonder whether beauty can come any other way. Would Pentecost?

Throughout this pilgrimage the images of the dead have been with me. "Of course," Sigmund Freud would respond, since journeys are universal symbols of death. I have continually reached back to the past, mine and the past of those I know in books. For them I have not needed death masks; they do not come to me from the grave. The disciples. The early Christian fathers. The ancient pilgrims. King Arthur. All dead. Yet living, present. Living somehow in my vision of pilgrimage, as they have come to me warm and whole, not cold or crumbling beneath my fingers. They have come to show us what pilgrimage means, a walk to death and beyond. Finally, I can write, finally I have reached the greatest tension point in pilgrimage, that longing for life in the midst of death, that hatred of death in the love of life: living leads to death and dying in order to live. As I read and reread the words on this page, they sound too facile. Translated into living texts—or dying ones—the story becomes a language I cannot speak or read so fluently.

How often we reenact the past in living the present, even a past that we create as we live the present. Each holy day we celebrate, each holy place we visit, each sin we repent and ask penance for—all have been done before. We merely repeat the actions of others, and much of what we see are their tombs: circles, returning yet again. Even the church ruins that once held living worship are emblematic graveyards of the dead that I must people with pulse and heartbeat. Must. My feeble attempt to bring life into the midst of rotting beams and weed- and rodent-infested churchyards. Perhaps this need to bring back the dead lives in all of us who seek monuments, museums, ancient trails and pathways. Look at what the dead wrought, we say. Or perhaps we gloat, instead, that we live and they have rotted, forgetting that someday others will stand in our place and gloat in much the same way. How short-lived is such triumph.

All this I face because I somehow missed my pilgrimage through Pentecost. But if it hadn't been Pentecost it would have been some other holy day, some other reality that forced me to look inward to see what makes me so restless, so angry, so hungry for something beyond what I see and touch. My senses are not enough, not nearly enough. David knew it: David the shepherd, David the singer, David the king, David the adulterer. All the Davids he was, all the Davids he tried to understand in all the psalms he wrote, all driven by the same longing, even his adultery the result of the fundamental passion for joy and life that his life had begun to deaden. He could not find his peace in being an *every day kind of man.*

These are Thomas Hardy's words. An every day

kind of man. An every day kind of woman. The search for meaning, purpose, identity, definition—pilgrimage. Is that what it really means—simply to be an every day kind of person? What solidity and comfort those words have. Plain, ordinary, oak-made. An every day kind of person takes the path as it comes, regardless. Regardless of giants or dragons, rocks or cliffs. An every day kind of person perseveres, not with grim determination, though sometimes we need that, but perseveres with humor and steadfastness. And enthusiasm.

In writing these words I am again condemning myself, though I am good at persevering; it's the humor and the enthusiasm I lack. Not all of the time, of course, for, as I said, I know moments when the joy of the journey overwhelms me. Those times make me eager to be on my feet, pitting my strength—my weakness?—against the path that lives beneath me. Such a gift of clarity is to be cherished, for too often perseverance is clouded by jealousy over another's success, or fear of failure, or anger at the imperfections around me. Yet *imperfections* is too weak a word, and sin is not entirely appropriate. Did my car sin when it refused to start, thus disturbing my plans and my peace and my concentration? It certainly is a sign of the imperfections I suffer with; it certainly is a sign of decay and death, for nothing, cars especially, lasts forever. Jealousy, fear, and anger, all interrelated. Like seats on a Ferris wheel, when one moves they all move.

But an every day kind of person, a pilgrim who walks in strength and serenity, who does what needs to be done the way Hardy's every day kind of man does, without complaint, never rides that Ferris wheel, another image of the circles that spin us dizzy. But even he, that every day kind of man, will die, mourned by those who understood his virtues, ignored by those who didn't, one day forgotten, as we all will be forgotten, until someone with a penchant for old graveyards brushes away the weeds and dust to read the now-faint letters of his serviceable headstone and recreates his life in a moment of fancy.

Allen and I saw many such serviceable headstones in the churchyards we visited, graves and grace sharing the same space. We don't do that anymore, bury people in the churchyard—not enough ground, I suppose, it being taken up by more important things like blacktop, a graveyard for fossil fuel and not human beings whose lives centered on the building next door. But to worship near the dead seems more appropriate than near a lot filled with Hondas and Chevys. The clouds of witnesses, the communion of the saints, seems much more present to me when I must cross a graveyard to enter the living presence of God. Or perhaps it is simply more of a comfort to me, a physical embodiment of what the Church assures me is so.

There are two kinds of churches that keep their dead close—cathedrals where prelates' bones lie in crypts and undercrofts and rulers rest in marble boxes, their effigies covering them. And tourists by the hundreds of thousands parade by them each year, marveling at how short was Henry VIII or how high the forehead of his—bald?—daughter, Elizabeth. They count the poets and read a few lines of Milton or Wordsworth and wonder whether they stand on poets' graves. This is one kind of church. Westminster Abbey. Canterbury Cathedral and the resonances of Thomas à Becket. Great events still occur in those places—weddings, baptisms, funerals. Coronations. Rituals of power.

Then there is the other kind of church, the kind whose front path into the narthex cuts through graves of rough marble I clutch for reassurance as I walk toward the red door. One. Two. Three. On my left; on my right. My feet shuffle forward with the help of these stones, a walker for young and old. That kind of church draws me from the street, into its yard, and up its few stairs, even on Sundays when I, away from home and community, might as easily stay put. It smells old and looks musty. Yet great events too still take place within its walls. Weddings. Baptisms. Funerals. But no coronations. No great and dead rulers. No Thomases, More or Becket. No political or ideological connections at all to attract any but the pilgrim seeking solace, refuge, and sense out of a life lived to die. A retreat from the maggots and decay to enable us to confront them nobly, and live.

I have visited both kinds of churches in Great Britain and in Europe. I recall sitting in a German pastry shop, drinking the kind of deep black coffee I cannot duplicate in my kitchen and eating some kind of rich cake, what kind I no longer recall but probably almond. I still see myself, at a narrow table next to a window near the front of the thin shop, a space unaffected by its own calories. It was dusk and I was writing, a journal I still have, somewhere.

I was recording the oppression of the Cathedral above me. It seemed that in one city after another I recorded the same oppression, though each city offered a different physical representation. Here its walls were so close that had the window been open on that bleak October afternoon I could have touched its gray walls. Germany seldom sees the sun in October, but this pastry shop, nearly attached to the glowering Cathedral, would always live in shadow, thanks to the Cathedral tower. I had not yet visited the sanctuary to learn whether it lived up to its name, though there in the pastry shop writing of it I felt only suffocation, not sanctuary, from its four walls.

It wasn't a large Cathedral as Cathedrals go—nothing like Cologne or Canterbury—but the steps to its famous tower, famous for what I don't know, were worn deep in the center, and dangerous, as the caretaker as well as the tower sign warned. I wanted to reach the top, a mountaineer's urge, but the narrow twisting and turning of the irregular stone defeated me, especially when no longer protected by walls, when the tower opened. Looking back, it appears more dangerous to me than the narrow paths above the sea or the mist-blinding moors. No, I found no sanctuary.

Only the small, insignificant, falling-down churches offer that protection. I recall that beside one, which was certainly in need of structural shoring up, stood sections of the Roman wall, but whether we were inside the City or outside it I do not recall. The streets we walked and the sixteenth- and seventeenth-century maps I later studied in the map room of the British Library refuse to overlap. At the time it seemed unimportant whether I was excluded or included, within the city walls or without; now, looking back, it seems crucial to know. For outside the walls lay the Liberties, places of marginalized society—brothels, lazar houses, the public theaters. How could I tell whether this eighteenth-century church grew up within society or outside of it, for the Liberties had disappeared, a transient cultural phenomenon, one that would have seemed out of place in an ordered, respectable, middle-class society. So the Liberties had long since disappeared, no longer performing any ritual, social function when the cornerstone for this parish church was put in place. Neverthe-less, the City walls remain, even today, an anachronism. The disguise of progress may make the stones hard to spot, but they are there.

Once again I am back to the dead—the living dead, the restlessly moving pilgrims hoping for miracles and cures: the pariahs of society shut out and yet celebrated by a ritual feast of shutting out that parish and priest enforced on these pariahs. Only this time I do not see worshipers rising and falling within a yellow Cotswold church or monks making their treacherous way along the Cornish coast. Those living dead, however marginal to our own culture, were central to theirs. The ones I see now had no place within society. Leprosy condemned them to leave spouse and children and trade; leprosy remitted them from work and responsibility.

In the Middle Ages lepers had roamed the country-side ringing a bell to announce their disease and identity, but in the Renaissance lepers were ceremonially con-ducted to the Liberties, to the lazar houses, the leprosari-ums—not for healing but for containment. There is something to be said for a society that creates an outer space to confine all that it considers immoral, diseased, evil. The assumption is that those who live within the walls are untainted by the evils included outside the walls. We know how faulty the assumption, then or now. Living within the walls does not make me any less diseased, only less obvious, like someone who harbors the AIDS virus for years before seeing any of its physical manifestations. So all that a leper represented seems emblematic of pilgrim-age: people who know themselves to be the living dead; who know our need of healing, not merely of contain-ment; who know that without the intervention of grace each breath brings us closer to our last. But grace does intervene.

The ceremony conducting lepers from the city to the Liberties melded the physical and the metaphysical. A prelate read the service for the dead—the burial service—with the corpse, only accidentally still breathing, the primary parishioner present. Not that he was alone. All the parish turned out, not wanting to miss any festival, no matter how macabre it strikes us today. The people knew that marking life or death in ritual was fundamentally necessary to community. By making the dismissal of lepers a religious ceremony, a festive, holy day, the parish ensured the living dead a centrality to its life, despite the resultant installation into a lazar house outside the City walls and so outside the community.

A strange paradox, making someone central and yet marginal simultaneously. The seeming contradiction meets, however, in the nature of the burial service; rather than mourning for the dead it celebrates the Resurrection, the fact that though we die we live. The act of death is also the act of birth, rebirth. Not everyone is so privileged as to appear at his own funeral service. Not everyone has the opportunity to rehearse her own death. Such privilege came only to lepers, because their disease proclaimed them dead. Which also, through the festal celebration of Resurrection, proclaimed them alive. Eternally alive. For the rest of the community, for the rest of us, our death does not speak so stridently, nor does our life speak so exultantly.

Lepers, picaros, pilgrims. We need such a ceremony that not only inters the body but asserts its resurrection. For none of us belongs within the City walls but all of us find our rightful place in the Liberties, a spatial metaphor we can't quite fit into our late twentieth-century society. Once instituted, it was controlled by no governor or law but existed through its own marginality, which allowed it to look on society and proclaim its foolishness, question its justice, interrogate its systems and institutions.

The Liberties served, in part, the role of prophet, a role every society needs yet none wants. Prophets themselves don't always find their robes easy to wear, for a prophet's image is wild, maniacal, even bestial. His words seem mad to the seemingly sane and ordinary discourse inside the city walls, so much so that some residents cannot understand the language, any more than Don Quixote's words made sense to those he encountered. He spoke from one culture while the people heard from another.

Are we any different? We don't fit, we don't belong, we can't be anything but marginal to the concerns of a culture that regards holy days and holy places as irrelevant, or worse, imaginary. Because that makes us like a leper, we sit outside the city wall or wander the countryside ringing our bell, a strange oxymoron, calling attention to something that everyone wants to recognize once, and then ignore.

And where does the church fit? I ask myself. The question nags at me, forcing me to return again and again to the parish church we visited in the north of London. Would it be within the walls or within the Liberties, wherever the Liberties are to be found, however they are configured, literally as in the Renaissance or metaphorically as today?

Walls protect, or they imprison; they exclude as well as include. But most of the time we don't think of what is included *outside* the walls, because our spatial perceptions, and our linguistic understanding of the circumstances of space, make the words *inside* and *include* parallel each other, *outside* and *exclude* the parallel antonyms. In other words, we don't envision ourselves outside the walls, looking around us to see what the outside includes. When we talk of pilgrims and lepers, of social centers and social margins, of acceptable space and licensed space, such as the Liberties were, our common notions of inside and outside, include and exclude simply fail to be sufficient.

Becoming a pilgrim radicalizes our point of view— an ugly neologism but one that serves to sharpen our focus. Pilgrims can no longer see themselves inside the walls. Rather, they must see themselves as citizens of the Liberties, excluded from the inside and thus included in the outside.

This reversal between inside-outside, excludeinclude existed just as much in Jesus' day as it did in the Renaissance, and as it does now. Jesus saw the invisible walls between the clean and the unclean, though he was not unique in this regard. The ability to tell the clean from the unclean was a mark of community; any member of Jewish culture would be able to do what Jesus could do. But Jesus reinterpreted the meaning. The unclean, the people Jewish culture marginalized, whether lepers, whores, or women with uncontrollable menses: These people of the invisible Liberties were included in the equally invisible Kingdom of God. What the walls excluded God included; what the walls included God excluded. And outside became inside in a radical violence against the logic of language and the society defined by those who are inside and those who are outside. What the walls of every society seek to keep out, or to keep people from, God seeks to keep in. Those inside the City walls are the ones in prison; those outside the walls are the ones at liberty. Once you know yourself to be dead, to be lacking in everything society considers necessary for life and liberty, as Solzhenitsyn has said, *then* and only then are you alive and free.

Jesus chose to live outside the walls and within the metaphoric Liberties of his culture. He haunted the lazar houses, the brothels, the public playhouses; and those should also be the haunts of the church, which should do more than offer a ritual service to exile the dead. The church should go with the dead into exile; the living have no need of resurrection. And as the church is merely a collection of pilgrims we will find ourselves wandering outside the walls, through marble headstones and crude crosses, past the graves of our ancestors to our own tombs and so beyond the fear of death to the joy-filled fact of life. It is a trip to Bountiful.

Nearing the End

....

The hunger for home is so strong that we search all our lives for its geography. Even when we are where people would name *home,* something tells us "not so." It is merely an accidental resting place, a waystation, a rocky shelter along the dusty trail. We have not reached Bountiful. A pilgrim truly committed to the trip will try anything to get there, even sneaking off without money or resources, defying those who tell her Bountiful no longer exists—and never did. I recently watched Horton Foote's award-winning film, *A Trip to Bountiful,* which is about a dying woman who escapes from her son and daughter-in-law to return to Bountiful, her home. She will not die peacefully until she breathes once more the peace of Bountiful—which has ceased to exist as a town, for its last citizen had just been buried.

A Trip to Bountiful reflects the trouble with literalizing geography. It may be hard to map a metaphor or a Kingdom that we can't see but yet have been assured exists, but Bountiful or Terre Haute or Tucson, well, that's another story. That's the kind of geography that maps well. We can pull out an atlas, open to the page marked Southeast Texas, and say, "Nope. No Bountiful." For most of us, that's the only kind of map we ever read, one that has roads and highways clearly marked, with all the big towns boldfaced, the kind you can navigate a car by. As if the only way to travel is by gasoline engine. But there are maps and geographies where no car can take us. Isn't that the kind of place Bountiful is? Rand McNally can't print directions for it or tell us how to understand it when we find it, wherever we find it—here on earth or in our imagination and spirit.

Bountiful is just another name for pilgrimage, a place we've got to reach that seems foolish to hardheaded tourists who only travel to the well-known and the highly reputed, like Paris or the giant redwoods of California. Bountiful. What's a Bountiful? Its very name is contradiction, a place that isn't a place but a journey, which lacks everything that *bountiful* stands for. Here's another word that has traveled far from its early meanings, like holiday and holy day. To see bountiful we must look with the vision of Don Quixote, not the eyes of Anne Tyler's Macon Leary, who would have us travel smart and quick, not long and messy. Macon Leary wants to travel without change or inconvenience; he wants no experience to mark us. Macon Leary wouldn't write an *Accidental Tourist* guidebook for Bountiful. For one thing, it's just too difficult to get there; tourists like the life of easy travel.

But life holds lots of Bountifuls, places along the road with nothing but sand and weeds and filling stations, places away from the center, or what people would have us believe is the center. Those places, those Bountifuls, are places of tender mercies, where Grace forms and transforms transience to permanence, weeds to wildflowers. We may land in such a marginal existence quite by accident; we may even get there because we're mired in sin, to use an old expression. Like Mack Sledge in Foote's other film *Tender Mercies,* we wake up from a lifetime drunk, need a job, take to fixing a few things around the place, and find out that the place has fixed us. Next thing we know we're being baptized, a kind of ritual burial service, our invisible leprosy scoured clean. C. S. Lewis's Eustace Scrubb, in *Voyage of the "Dawn Treader,"* shedding his dragon skin all over again. Like Sledge some of us are wise enough to realize what's happened and admit the change is long overdue; some of us willingly accept the path pilgrimage offers right away. Although I'd like to say I was one of those, I can't.

Growing up I wanted tourism, I wanted vacations, I wanted time off, I wanted escape. But I never wanted pilgrimage. Pilgrimage—that was something permanent, something you never returned from. Vacations, on the other hand, smelled of Samsonite glamour, richly tanned. Their reality came in the weight of the carefully packed trunks and the cost of the short-lived ticket. A person could get a lot of mileage out of a vacation without a lot of commitment. Or so I thought when I was a teenager, my head stuffed with too many stories of upperclass travel. I lived with visions, all right, but not the kingdom kind or those of Don Quixote. Righting wrongs and serving justice had no appeal.

But my mother thought differently. Tourism was— well—for tourists, which we weren't. Nor did my mother intend us to be, ever. We were on a different kind of life journey, or at least she was, which caused lots of friction. I resented never spending a few weeks on a lake or a month in the mountains, as my friends did. If even that sort of vacation was beyond me, I knew I could never aspire to summers in Providence or touring on the Continent, stocking my mind with memories while I filled diary after diary with beautiful, precocious prose. My modern-day paraphrase of *Pilgrim's Progress*, a birthday present from my grandmother, which I dutifully and loyally read as I read all the books anyone ever gave me, didn't have the romantic draw as did the books I picked for myself from lemon-oiled library shelves. Although the Slough of Despond was dramatic and Vanity Fair tantalizingly wicked, they weren't the paths for me.

I read too much and too indiscriminately; I see that now, just as I see myself wandering in the old Carlisle library: Carlisle, Pennsylvania, home of Dickinson College and not much else. But the library is something to recall, with its high ceilings, paneled walls, permanent, wood bookcases. No metal in sight. A trip to the library for me was a trip to Bountiful, a bountiful I hadn't remembered until now, just as I hadn't realized the weaknesses of my reading. Although my mother disagreed about vacations, she and I saw eye to eye about libraries. So I got to visit my Bountiful often, though I guess not often enough, since I supplemented my Carlisle supply with stash from the school library and my mother's own supply. Recalling the adult books I read at far too early an age made me cautious with my stepchildren, so that I read what they read. Just to make sure. When it came to books, I see that my mother was more liberal-minded than I.

But books provided the vacations she denied me: I *used* them. They also revealed what I was really being denied—not glamour but the *memories* of glamour. I would never be able to look back on a summer romance: moonlight, water, sand, heartbreaking goodbyes, promises of fidelity if only through letters. I would never be able to recall that one summer when I left school an ugly duckling and returned to school a white-winged swan, a longing, I suspect of many teenagers trapped in the in-betweens. Or maybe it is the permanent condition of most of us, a condition that propels us into pilgrimage. We want to connect the inside of us to what shows on the outside; we need to find the geography between the inside and the outside where we exist. But back then in my fifteen-year-old arrogance I thought the in-betweens were the coin of teenagers only. I would never be able to return to that certain cabin where I had journeyed into what life meant, because I lacked a Maine lake or a Golden Pond to visit or revisit. I could not return, as Reynolds Price does in *Tongues of Angels,* to a summer camp in the Blue Ridge Mountains. I didn't even have Disneyland.

What bothered me most, though, was a sense that I needed such memories, or something like them, because I was going to be a Writer. Capital W. My sister already was a Writer. Hadn't she produced a manuscript called *The Ulcered Few,* a wry, trenchant look at her life in the eighth grade? Hadn't a publisher almost accepted it? Too short, they said, after considering it for several months. I had started a book, longhand, a pastiche of Mary Stewart's *The Moonspinners,* which I had just finished, and Nancy Drew. My best friend had even read what I'd written. Although she liked it, I had sense enough to recognize pastiche and so quit writing; no doubt I've grown less discriminating and more tolerant of my faults with age.

Anyway, I'd read enough to realize that Writers needed memories, or Memory, though the abstract, capitalized concept was probably beyond me then. What would I do without some romantic events to remember? Where would my make-believe come from if I had no memories to make-believe *from?* Even today, even now when I recall the Carlisle library, I can't conjure up a colorful librarian. So here I am, unable to recall people or places of moment, but recognizing that when I asked for vacations I was really asking for something else. I wanted an inner pilgrimage, of which the movement from home to lake and back again was merely the luggage.

Lacking both inner pilgrimage and tourism, I stuck to books, hoping in some way to manufacture memories out of the make-believe of others. It seems that I do it still. Books were deceptively safe, since, as I said, my mother and I saw eye to eye about them. She read voraciously, constantly, and everywhere. No part of the house was safe from her invasion, no time the wrong time for a book. I followed her lead; what she read, I read, from Agatha Christie to Dorothy L. Sayers, Christie by the time I was twelve, Sayers by the time I was sixteen. I read books she had read in her twenties, like *See Here Private Hargrove* and *My Life with Father*. Nonfiction written like fiction, though I claimed I didn't like true stories. I read books from her childhood, the *Anne of Green Gables* books by L. M. Montgomery passed down to me from my grandmother to my mother. My mother's copy of *Little Women* and *Eight Cousins, The Old-Fashioned Girl*, and *The SWF Club*—the See Winston First Club. I was especially fond of that one because the main characters, like me, had no place to go in the summer.

Those books were pretty tame stuff. Although I loved to cry over Matthew's death in *Anne of Green Gables* or the death of Beth in *Little Women*, and used to reread just those sections to make myself cry, like rehearsing a part I knew I would one day play when I lost a boyfriend, the only kind of death I thought would ever come my way, I also needed something stronger. Stephen King was still working his own way through high school, but I had other, riskier choices: *The Tropic of Cancer*, which I read by covered flashlight; *Peyton Place*, a perfect size to fit inside my biology book; and *Lady Chatterly's Lover*, just the dirty parts, the only parts of any Lawrence novel I have ever read. None of these came from the austere Carlisle library, and certainly not from the school library. A tenth-grade English teacher had found himself in front of a special school board meeting for assigning *Catcher in the Rye*. We had a private circulating library, strange now that I think about it but something I accepted as naturally as I accepted the other libraries in my life. Where else would I get such books except from another student?

And so I read the interesting parts of Lawrence one night at a school dance. My mother objected to dancing on other grounds; I'm certain it never occurred to her that I might *read* something wicked in the school gym. Teachers who served as chaperones had their eyes out for students necking in the corners, not sitting bold and unashamed with a book in hand. Would they have recognized it as a dangerous and potentially more subversive act? Either there weren't many dirty parts, or I was a fast reader, because I took in Lawrence while "Can't Help Falling in Love" and "Big Girls Don't Cry" played over the loud-speaker and Nield Whitmore looked for someone else to display his dance skill with.

But no story satisfied my longing for memory, so night after night before falling asleep I made up my own—stories or memories, I'm not sure which I thought I was doing. Often I was the heroine, but just as often I made up a heroine and set her in motion, stupid and trivial stories, so that I could watch and listen, especially the latter. My head was near bursting with dialogue. Even today I hold long, mental conversations with myself or with others; it makes for a noisy life. And confusing. I remember voices so clearly that at times I'm uncertain whether I've held a conversation with someone or simply conducted it in my head.

Given how much I longed for travel, I don't know why I refused it once I was on my own, though by then I had grown accustomed to taking my trips secondhand and found the habit hard to break. Nor did the exhaustion I saw on my friends' faces after vacations encourage me to do so. Opening a book was quicker, cheaper, and more relaxing than packing and unpacking numerous times during a whirlwind week of tourism. Anne Tyler had not yet written Macon Leary's advice into existence. Gradually, though, I decided that secondhand scenery, no matter how skilled the second *hand* was with words, could only go so far. I wanted to see what I had been reading about since I deciphered my first word. But on *my* terms— no tours, no charts, no schedules, no buses, and no "see Great Britain in three days or less."

If I had decidedly un-tourist-like ideas about travel by then, I nevertheless viewed my passport with awe. I still do. It seemed a great and special feat to have achieved such a document; not even my father, who spent twenty years in the Navy and traveled everywhere, had a passport. When he finally needed one for a trip to Vietnam as a civilian working for the Navy department, the government had to overlook his lack of a birth certificate, the result of a small, Southern oversight. I didn't understand it—he was *here*, wasn't he? He'd served in World War II, hadn't he? Ah, but was he American, that was the question. Illegal aliens could have crafty disguises.

A passport is such a precious document and comes with such warnings about keeping it safe that I have never taken it for granted—unlike my social security card, which I lost long ago. When I need special legal identification, I open my file marked "passport." I have another for documents and certificates where I file my birth record, along with the warranty for my refrigerator and my KitchenAid hand mixer, but my passport requires its own folder.

But it isn't only *my* passport that fascinates me. Waiting in airports, I always hope for a look at the passports from other countries. A U.S. passport is small compared with passports from Great Britain, France, or Canada—almost insignificant, insubstantial. Heathrow is the airport for a passport-studier. Sitting in our favorite coffee shop there, having a last scone before boarding our flight, I wonder what people think when I stare from table to table, searching for a glimpse into another country, for a passport as much as clothing or language stamps a culture. It seems an emblem of the country itself, the way it would be known to others. It puzzles me that so many countries choose drab colors—olive green or brown; why not red? Their airlines would not be so insensitive. My shiny, navy blue passport, despite its size stands out against the lackluster passports of other countries. It is assertive, just like most Americans, I suppose, who assert more than they should when waiting at Heathrow or Frankfurt or when staying at a bed and breakfast.

We no longer expect to meet American tourists; when we do we wonder whether all of them carry Leary's *Accidental Tourist* with them. They seem so little affected by the culture they have invaded, or I should say cultures, because no country, not even ours, consists of one culture only. So pilgrims discover different cultural assumptions when they travel to the north of England or to the southwest. The same is true in Germany. In the south, Munich for instance, breakfast means a hard roll and coffee, perhaps some liverwurst; at ten o'clock the coffee shops fill with customers ordering blood sausage. No one has a table to herself; whoever needs a seat takes it. But in the north, around Frankfurt or Cologne, breakfast is a full meal—three-minute eggs, meat, rolls, coffee, and more, just as it is in most parts of the U.K. A cooked breakfast, to distinguish it from cold cereal only, though a cooked breakfast begins with cereal. Depending on location, a guest might also get fried bread and mushrooms in addition to ham and sausage, toast, eggs, and grilled tomato. A breakfast in Britain equals my normal, daily caloric intake. At Holdstone Farm, where Jane served breakfast with a flourish, we encountered the assertive American tourists we had only read about.

The rituals of B and Bs vary as much as the food can. In some, the hostess tells you the time of breakfast; in others you tell her when you will appear at table. In either case, you should not fail to appear at the proper time, not early, not late. When you request your food—coffee, tea, cooked breakfast, no cooked breakfast—you stick with your choice. And if you are particular about your coffee, as I am, you soon learn to ask whether it is filtered, the opposite being instant. If instant, I request tea.

On this particular morning, we appeared as usual, and a few minutes later Jane entered the dining room to find out what we wanted. As we were the only guests, we were surprised to find a second table laid. Jane explained that some other Americans had arrived the evening before and would be down soon. That's when the problems started. The party of five straggled down one at a time. The first one ordered a cooked breakfast, as did the second, who changed her mind when it arrived. But then changed it back again when her husband's eggs enticed her. They violated the rituals, trying to transport American behavior to Exmoor. They were no less violent in their attack on the land, despite their claims that they wanted to see the country. See it, of course, from a car—a day for Dartmoor, an afternoon for Exmoor, an hour or two for Cornwall. Their navy blue and gold passports privileged them, so they thought, to consume the country rather than allow it to invade their culture.

A pilgrimage, even one permitted by political and social ideologies that a passport represents, reshapes the pilgrim. There is no packing the assumptions and expectations of the original culture along with our underwear and dried prunes. Accepting a passport implies a paradoxical willingness to dispense with the culture the passport presumes; it becomes, in the metaphoric terms of this pilgrimage, an exchange of one kingdom for another. At times it might be easier to distinguish our country of origin from our kingdom destination if we were issued a passport to Bountiful along with our political passport. We could hold it, study it, compare it to the passport destination of others. It would be a concrete way of identifying fellow pilgrims, and not so liable to confusion and mistaken identity. But Bountiful issues no such documentation, so pilgrims muddle along as best they can, learning that the discovery of like-destined walkers is part of the culture of that country, as much as navy blue passports and fried eggs is part of another.

"Then people long to go on pilgrimages." Geoffrey Chaucer was right. I suddenly had this longing, but on my terms, as I said. But since I said that three pages back I have written myself into contradicting that statement. *My* terms? There is no such thing on a pilgrimage. A pilgrim can't travel on her own terms or on any terms other than those the pilgrimage sets, which is different for each pilgrim, because the master pilgrim knows the road each of us needs to travel. In true twentieth-century fashion, I was unprepared for the road. No, more than that, I was startled that I wanted to be on any road, prepared or not. But after years of reading *about*, I wanted to find out for myself; reading was no longer sufficient but required, I was surprised to learn, commitment. And I believed that a commitment to walk in Britain paralleled or reflected or embodied my commitment to another kind of walk, that the two, the physical and the spiritual, met and served one another. I wanted to walk the same paths as those prodigious hikers William and Dorothy Wordsworth. I wanted to know whether the rumors of Dartmoor mists were true. I wanted bracken under foot and eye. I wanted sheep and heather. I longed for pilgrimage. Here, near the end of this pilgrimage, I return to the beginning to declare what set me on the path, the knowledge that second-hand pilgrimage was insufficient; I couldn't inherit it through print or parentage of any kind. This text had to become a living text for me, or it was no text at all.

Sooner or later, every pilgrim discovers that the spiritual and the physical are inseparable: the gift of the Incarnation, the seal of the Resurrection. What I do and where I go matters, matters on every level of existence, not just on the physical, which is the point of the walk. Although I am a slow learner, at least I am learning. In pilgrimage I cannot use the past perfect, for I *have not learned*—not yet, probably not ever. I am forced to reiterate Montaigne: "I have nothing to say entirely, simply, and with solidity of myself without confusion [and] disorder, blending, mingling," for "the more I frequent and know myself . . . the less I understand myself." And so it has been here; the more I frequent this bound-book universe the less certain I am that I pursue unambiguous truth, a straight line. I suspect that Montaigne speaks for all of us, not just for me. But we keep walking, for that is the condition of pilgrimage. We keep frequenting—visiting—ourselves to sort out the confusion and disorder, to come to some understanding of who we are and where we belong. Our mental journey inward is reflected by our physical journeys.

Looking back, it seems so natural, my discovery that walking was important. It gave the cliché "thinking on my feet" a new vision. My husband and I discovered this together, and together we were unprepared, either physically or spiritually. We had no boots, no raingear, no backpacks, no maps. Pilgrims in the Middle Ages wouldn't start as unprepared as we were, but perhaps, finally, I see that our foolish, twentieth-century approach to pilgrimage is closer to that of the first century than I originally assumed. Hadn't Jesus said, "Leave your nets and follow me"? Hadn't Jesus said, in so many words, "If you've got to get ready, then you aren't ready and won't ever be?" We have no time to feed the kids or bury our dead—or plow and plant the garden before making a last-minute stop at the discount sporting-goods store for a weatherproof jacket. We might have envied other walkers their knickers, their boots, their blister-proof layers of socks, but at least we were walking.

Our first day in Derbyshire changed us; only later did we understand what had happened. A 50-pence pamphlet with charming and irritating instructions for various walks of interest became as necessary as the verses we argued about in our Tuesday night Bible study. Only here we were arguing in the middle of cow pastures or halfway up a fell. Even when we knew what we were looking for, or so we thought, we managed to miss it, like the stile in a stone fence on our way to High Cup in the Pennine Mountains. Only after we had overlooked it and had retraced our steps did we see it—so obvious from one angle of vision, so invisible from the other. These directions were as open to interpretation, or should I say misinterpretation, as anything in Scripture. And like the Bible, our 50-pence pamphlets only made sense once we were on the other side of the directions, so that we said, regularly, "Oh, *now* I see what that meant."

To be fair to ourselves, our confusion wasn't always self-induced. We didn't always match Don Quixote in his continual misapprehensions—an ass for a grey palfrey, a barber's bucket for a blazing helmet. Occasionally, a disgruntled farmer subverted the footpath signs. We first heard about such things in the Cotswolds on our way to a particular village. Some local walkers warned us of the potential problems on the path, a lovely walk, certainly, but not one they would any longer recommend. The farmer didn't like walkers. Having made our way through barnyards, herds of cattle, and back pastures, having stopped to ask pilgrim permission at a farmhouse that seemed to be inhabited almost exclusively by large, angry dogs and received a friendly "Go ahead, you'll love the walk to Dartmeet," we were shocked to find a farmer who didn't want us.

"Took down the footpath signs," clipped a trans-
planted Scot.

"But that's illegal," I said.

"So it is. County made him put the signs back up.
But he put 'em up wrong."

"Wrong?"

I couldn't understand. The right of walkers to roam
on private property is common privilege, dating back
centuries when the only roads to market and church
rambled through farmland. It takes a lengthy legal process
to divert a public footpath. We had encountered one or
two, with signs stating the new law and the location of the
new footpath, sometimes one that paralleled the old
closely but now avoided a barnyard or pasture. A footpath
never disappeared altogether. We had also encountered a
sign or two that read, "Private. No Public Footpath,"
which contradicted the latest ordnance survey map, as
well as generations of common use. Finally I understood.
These signs were illegal, an initiative of the farmer, not the
result of a law. The problem, we have since learned
through a story in *The Wall Street Journal,* has become so
bad that walkers and farmers find themselves glaring at
each other across a courtroom. But that day in the
Cotswolds we knew nothing of pitched, legal battles.
After we thanked the locals for the warning, we continued
our climb.

That day the farmer won. We walked and walked,
our map and compass in hand, but a missing footpath
sign, another turned round, and several "No Access"
signs reinforced by barbed-wire fences, hemmed us in and
forced our path to fall where we did not want it to go. We
descended a hill into a condominium development at the
end of a small village that bumped into the Cotswold

pasture. A development? Of condominiums? We thought we had walked right back to the U.S., a confusion of footpath signs indeed. It took us some little while to figure out where we were and where we weren't. It was more than a little disconcerting, even for people as experienced at losing the way as we were, to learn that despite warnings and maps and compasses we had fallen into that farmer's trap and walked his path, not ours.

Back to Montaigne, back to Don Quixote, back to Paul. Back to being misled, despite our best intentions. This time it didn't matter, though we regretted the village we lost while enjoying the one we found, once, that is, we left the development behind. We aren't always so fortunate, however, when people shift the signs or subvert the path. Changing a word here or there can have great consequences for pilgrims—like holy day and holiday.

But other changes, other shifts in signs, have deadlier consequences. Devaluing words might matter more than a shift in definition: a public footpath that becomes private, where public no longer means what it once did. The word chastity has experienced this same devaluation. Once the word was common, meaning that it was used frequently, for even the word common has become ambiguous. "I cannot keep the subject still," said Montaigne, writing in French, a double problem for us who write in English, a language of thousands more words shifting under our fingers in a duplicitous and subversive fashion.

How can we keep the subject still, when the subject is pilgrimage, which in itself moves, and when the medium for the subject is so befuddled? But that is what we must take, as in *accept*, regardless of the difficulties, pilgrimage that eludes and confuses us, even while we are in the midst of it. Common—ordinary, everyday, typical. Common—cheap, tawdry, sexually suspect. Common chastity. Uncommon chastity. How chaste are we? Why chastity at all?

We have encountered it or its opposite, lust, as an aside in *Pilgrim's Progress*, a throwaway reference to Vanity Fair. But Christian struggled with lust in the city of Vanity Fair, much as he struggled with the Slough of Despond at the very start of his journey. Lust and Death arrive together, blood relatives, doubly incestuous. Sin is Satan's daughter as well as his bride, as Milton has shown us; the son of Sin, named Death, is also her lover. We know how insatiable a lover he is. Worst of all, we sleep with ourselves, lusting after and stroking our own bodies and souls to eternal damnation.

But lust is not merely sexual, not merely common. Lust encompasses all overweening attitudes, all opposites of chastity. I desire so many things that I am hard pressed to know where to begin to describe the extent of my longings. At times my lusts make me stagger under their weight. If I saw myself emblematized as medieval art, I would sicken from fright. I am being sucked dry by sin.

Am I chaste when I lust after money, or place, or name? Can my body be chaste when my soul is promiscuous? Death plays upon my lust in a fool's game. To lust seems so alive that we forget it is the mask of death. To succumb to lust, despite its intensity and pretense at life, is to embrace that which we have been fleeing—a maze we're running with the whispers of Sin's Lover shoving us in his direction by massaging the pleasure center of our brain. Oh, how good it feels, so good that we beg for more.

"Certainly," Death says—"just sign this paper and I'll give you every pleasure you crave."

"Paper? Is that a contract? Don't be ridiculous. I know quite well whose story you're imitating. Faust. Christopher Marlowe had him sign in blood. But it had nothing to do with pleasure, did it? As I recall, Marlowe's Faust craved knowledge—ambitions of intellectual greatness. Anyway, stories aren't true. They're just . . . *stories*, made ups, pretends, lies."

But lies very like the truth. So long as we think Faust is pretend we don't really have to worry about the whispers, the contract, or the maze. Let's concentrate on the pleasure; that, at least, is real enough, because we can feel it.

When we reach that point, we're trapped, each running our own way, so that we threaten to collide into each other rather than link arms and hearts to find the way out. But there's a maze within the maze, even more subtle and dangerous, the maze that claims lust is only a personal problem. Only personal. If *I* am chaste, that's all pilgrimage requires of me. If only that were true, how much easier would the life of a pilgrim be, how much less complicated. I take care of myself; you take care of yourself; the guy across the street or around the next bend handles his own temptations to whatever lusts he is prone to. Everything neat and orderly. I like that.

But chastity and lust are not matters each of us can keep to himself. They become modifiers of corporations, governments, and institutions—even churches. They involve us corporately as well as personally, for cultures can be promiscuous, or cultures can be chaste. A pilgrim can become one or the other by where he chooses to linger along the walk. Although it is inevitable that, just like

Bunyan's Christian, our walk will take us to some unsavory places, we don't need to unshoulder our pack, find some nice property, sign a thirty-year mortgage, and move in, all the while thinking that we will continue the pilgrimage later, once the kids have grown but for now we need the money and the stability. It doesn't take long for our hard-won muscle tone to melt like ice cream under an August sky.

Something is wrong here. What does lust have to do with mortgages? And what do mortgages have to do with churches? Lust means sex or pornography, not a four-bedroom split-level with paneled family room, two cars in the garage, a fire in the fireplace, and a CD player, tape deck, 22-inch color TV, and a VCR in the den. It just doesn't. I won't let it. And don't tell me about people who live in cardboard boxes like the one my Magnavox stereo system came in. I can't cope with it. It's got nothing to do with me, nothing. If those people weren't so unchaste, if they didn't lust after booze or drugs or Dunkin' Donuts, they might be warm and dry too. Those people just don't know when to stop the party. There is such a thing as work, as responsibility. We've got to meet the mortgage. It's their own fault. I refuse to look at them.

Because in their face I find Death. In their face I find my own.

Maybe we should go back to the parish system. Parishes took care of their own—bag ladies and AIDS victims, unwed mothers and lepers. This social structure, its organization, showed the value system it proclaimed. Everyone was a member of a parish centered in church, and all roads led to and from that center. But what happens when a society cannot economically support its marginalized citizens, its leftovers? What happens when there are too many bastards born for a parish to feed and clothe?

If I don't like the indigent in one parish, I can always move to another parish in search of indigent I find more acceptable, what we sometimes call "the deserving poor." Or I can go to a parish that marches its lepers and pregnant women out of town and so out of sight and mind—a parish that turns Britomart, the knight of chastity, out along with them.

We can refuse to hear about the social demands made on pilgrims. It's easy enough to pick and choose with whom to make our pilgrimage and what we'll talk about along the way. But here comes Britomart, whether or not we want her, riding straight for us out of Edmund Spenser's peculiar sixteenth-century poem *The Faerie Queen*.

This is not supposed to happen. It's not *real*. Characters don't just leap out of the pages of one book and catapult themselves down two flights of stairs and into another. It's one thing to read "When the Dolls Came to Life" at the age of ten, or to watch Tom Baxter of the Chicago Baxters in *The Purple Rose of Cairo* jump off the screen and into Cecilia's arms, but we know perfectly well that there is a limit. Such things happen only with Woody Allen, not with normal people making their monthly payments.

But Britomart, the only female knight in Spenser's allegory, knows when she is needed. She represents and champions Chastity, the third of three crucial virtues (the other two are Holiness and Temperance). Chastity, says Spenser, is "that fairest virtue." How long has it been since we thought of Chastity as fair, beautiful, worth holding and beholding?

Britomart is looking at me, and she's making me uncomfortable. In my fancy, I can see her eyes through the visor. Disappointed, that's what they are. Disappointed that I have so little vision not to know that she fights for chastity no matter whose territory or what the circumstances. A pilgrimage is a pilgrimage; whether it's the sixteenth century or the twenty-first—what does it matter to her? She shudders to find men whipping women bloody for bearing a bastard. How could a parish do that to its own? Such behavior is a violation of the value system a parish represented. But parishes in the sixteenth century did just that. Chastity was a public problem, because it was an economic problem, which made it a political problem. Whipping is bad enough but to Britomart it's worse when people shove women out of doors to give birth on the road, just so the bastard doesn't become another burden on an already straining economy. And the men who fathered the children go unpunished.

This is starting to sound familiar, for we have analogous situations today—for instance, Christian hospitals in Haiti refusing AIDS patients, because they burden resources. So the hospitals stand empty. Sterile, but empty. Or nurses who want the patients they treat to be morally acceptable to them. As soon as promiscuity threatens the larger social order, when private collides with public, we demand government action. So AIDS, our version of too many bastards or lepers that a parish cannot or will not support, causes our Congress to dust off words like chastity and billboard them.

We need Britomart as much as Spenser's England did. Parishes. I guess they didn't work any better than our own system does. They celebrated people right into cardboard boxes, right into the Liberties. But pilgrims don't need to worry about such matters; that's what governments are for. Should we meet any leper-like creatures on the path, which is unlikely, for those sorts don't make pilgrim commitments, we'll take up the question of what we should do then. There's no sense in volunteering for hazard duty. Make the trip look good or we won't have any takers. Who wants to risk leprosy or AIDS? They brought it on themselves, anyway.

I hear an argument, one of those noisy conversations I mentioned earlier that my mind holds with me, or itself. One character has said, "Yes, but haven't you brought *your* deathdoom on yourself? You may not be dying of AIDS or leprosy or cirrhosis of the liver, but how does that change the fact that every twisted, lustful step you take brings you closer to the end? Why should those people be shoved to the margins, some of whom are certainly fellow pilgrims, while you live within the City? Appearances have nothing to do with pilgrimage, which you should have learned by now." What can I answer?

Back when we began to walk we didn't know that walking would lead us into such trails. I could easily have written *trials.* Maybe I should have; the simple inversion transposes one into the other and back again, a verbal Slinky toy. We didn't understand that pilgrimage would strip away all our pretensions to goodness to expose our lusts and fears. No wonder we're commanded to get going and ask questions later. No wonder that the New Testament image of the narrow road and the treacherous path demands, among other things, concern for the hungry, the desperate, the naked. Our companions are those society tosses out of the city walls.

Yet we find it nearly as hard to accept ourselves as it is to accept our fellow pilgrims, especially when we know that we don't look the part. For some reason we don't take people seriously when they violate appearances. We must have been an astonishing sight, my husband and I, as ludicrous to path-wise walkers as Ralph appeared to elite dog-owners. Picaros in appearance if not in name or in concern for social justice and ideological revolution. We had not yet learned, that day in Derbyshire when we walked to some deserted mines, a hearty roundtrip of twenty miles, that pilgrims will always appear foolish, despite their equipment. To become pilgrims is to link ourselves with people on the outside; to be out of step with culture is to be in step with a radical culture that refuses Pharisaical rules, which determine who is good enough and who isn't. We come to slowly realize that another set of rules is operating, using a system none of us quite understands.

Yet how foolish we felt in our Nikes, London Fogs, and umbrellas, as we waded knee-deep through a barley field under mine-black skies and sheets of rain. Yet we wanted to do it right, whatever that meant, though at the time we were thinking only of proper hiking boots and something to keep the insides dry. As if clothes would make us acceptable.

The next year we almost succeeded. At least we had the boots, socks, and packs, though I clung to my raincoat and carried my umbrella, convinced, I suppose, that we had not seen the worst the weather had to offer. I was wrong. That year we saw Dartmoor, Arthur Conan Doyle country—a small piece, the southeastern section, for four days of hard walking, daylight to dusk. We perfected our ability to lose our way, but somehow to find it again. It was also the year my husband realized his dream to fish in English waters, though you'll have to ask him to tell you that story.

We began to lose our way in Dartmoor from the very first mile, so that we arrived at our bed and breakfast at the awkward dinner hour and not mid-afternoon as we had planned. Our roadmap failed to record the threadlike lanes that tied the interior of Dartmoor to the motorways. We pulled into a village carpark and waited. Hungry, tired, and frustrated, we had all the makings, in other words, for a Dagwood-sized fight. Which proceeded along predictable lines—"It's your fault"; "No, it's your fault— you misread the map." Only the appearance of the owner of the small truck parked next to us stopped our invectives. Despite the fact that we could barely understand his English, we pieced together the instructions for our destination, a small village called Widdecombe. We also pieced together that we had come a deal of a way out of our way. A long, hard drive lay ahead. At least the high clouds and blue sky made for a pleasant backdrop to our bungling stage play.

Widdecombe, we learned the next morning, was a favorite stop for tour buses, despite the dangers of getting in and out, surrounded as it is by the steep Dartmoor tors—those rugged rocky hills. We disliked the tours but loved the tors, even the name, one of the few remnants of Welsh in our native English. Fortunately, the buses stopped only long enough to disgorge their contents onto waiting merchants selling postcards, knick-knacks, and a cuppa. We learned to avoid Widdecombe around 10 a.m.

I said Widdecombe was our destination when I should have said that Higher Venton Farm, two miles east of the village, was our actual destination. Although U.S.

Customs people don't like Americans to touch British farms—are they afraid we'll pick up hoof-and-mouth disease?—we prefer an agricultural setting. Maybe it's our desire to reach the ancient yeoman stock, to stroke the backbone of Great Britain. Or maybe we just enjoy cattle.

Peter Hicks greeted us in his barnyard with the cheerful news that we had seen the last of the good weather: storms moving in from Cornwall and he hoped we hadn't planned anything in the way of outdoor activity. Which, of course, was all we *had* planned. With a sigh, we hauled our two suitcases out of our rented, British-made Ford Fiesta, and entered a smallish farmhouse, walked through the dining-sitting room, climbed narrow, winding stairs, to greet one of the tiniest bedrooms we had encountered in the U.K. But it had a wash basin, so how could we complain?

That greeting was the last time Peter Hicks looked us in the eye—and not because he was shy.

Also staying at Higher Venton Farm, to distinguish it from Lower Venton Farm half a farm lane away, was a British family on holiday: half term and bank holiday combined. Peter Hicks preferred to look them straight and narrow, as if their presence reassured him that he wasn't always fated to guest foreigners. Even when forced to speak to us he kept his eyes securely and reassuringly clapped on his own kind. His own in national origin only, however. Our fellow guests were many generations removed from the farm, unlike us. We had spent part of our early years on a dairy farm, which Higher Venton was. My husband, in fact, had worked a farm so like this old, old Dartmoor land—only forty-eight acres, rocks, a few dozen head of cattle, black and white terriers. In upstate New York when he was a boy people still farmed with animals because tractors couldn't negotiate the contours of the land.

But none of that mattered. We were Americans, and Peter Hicks clearly hadn't much use for our kind, whether from personal experience or vicarious experience I couldn't tell, though not many of us would venture to such an out-of-the-way farm for four days of rigorous hiking in some of the foulest weather I will ever encounter. Maybe that was it. Maybe he considered us not quite right in the head. Maybe we weren't. Nevertheless, Peter Hicks fascinated me, one of the few remaining Dartmoor farmers, with all its resonances—few words, spoken thickly; small, wiry stature; a scrape-by existence; nightly trips to the local pub of a few hundred years' standing and nothing like the pubs of today.

Slowly, under my husband's patient, quiet questions, Peter Hicks revealed the history of Higher Venton Farm—his years as tenant farmer to the locally famous novelist Beatrice Chase, then his years playing nursemaid to her, and his accidental inheritance of the farm right after he had purchased one down the road. Contrary to Chase's reputation for charity, largely the result of the image she presented to the world through her books, she was hell on brogues, tormenting and mistreating workers and servants.

"You'd put nails in her fence for her and she'd hand you ten bob—a lot of money in the 40s. And as soon as yer back wor turned, she would try to put two nail between yer should blades. She wor as unpredictable and dicey as one of her favorite tors, all mist one moment and sunshine the next."

Peter Hicks stopped after that long speech and for a time would say no more.

Beatrice Chase, it appeared, played Peter Hicks with the skill of a consummate fly fisherman bringing home a wily brown trout. Seven times she rewrote her will, making him dizzy with his revolving in and out of the pages. She happened to die while he was in—a stroke of fortune or the Providence of God, he wasn't prepared to say which, though when her lawyer called with the news he refused to credit it. "Not," so he assured us, "that the inheritance was worth much, then or now." Only his family's long connection with the place, and his family's family time out of mind, memory out of mind, made him glad of the will, or so his pursed lips and shrugging shoulders led us to believe. Like tribes who still live by oral tradition, the British farmers we met live with memories hundreds of years old, memories that they hold, not merely stories they have been told. Grudges and feuds hold good. As he told his story, in disjointed bits and disconnected pieces during the four days and nights we lived with him, I too remembered the old days.

More than that, I hungered for those memories, as if that hunger and my hunger for home were the same. As if, could I stretch my memory back far enough, I'd reach the original memory of all of us, when we became human, learned our first words, took our first halting, lisping steps toward story and definition, when made-up became what we remembered because we had nothing prior to the beginning. I wanted to be Peter Hicks and his wife, I wanted to live when Beatrice Chase lived, to see it whole before my eyes and find the accent fall naturally off my tongue. Because her books filled the house, I read several, trying to locate her in the Higher Venton Farm I saw before me.

But this was recent history, twentieth-century history, a mere child of a story in the midst of the stories of those weeks spent between New Forest, Dartmoor, and back to New Forest. New Forest is a misnomer for those of us who understand new to mean what advertisers have just taken up. In 1066 the forest was new to William the Conqueror, the forest of giant beeches and oak. And so it is still new, though 1066 is old. No monarch since Charles II has kept house in New Forest, yet the old rules and rulers, the Verderers, the supreme court justices of New Forest law and lore, still hold court. Common law can win, so Jack Newman assured us, as we sat in Annie Cooper's glass-enclosed dining hall having tea. "We still have a little bit of fun, like," he said. Sharp-eyed and sharp-tongued, his pleasure was to best the Verderers, to study the family's ancient rights under common law, and to insist that they be honored, rights like that of common pasture on New Forest land or rights to firewood, called estovers.

To non-natives, New Forest is not well known, for when most people think of Great Britain, areas like the Cotswolds, Cornwall, or the great moors come first to mind. The legendary forest is that of Sherwood, of course, thanks to Robin Hood and his band of merry men who roamed during the reign of Richard and John, long after William conquered. The year we ventured to New Forest was the first we had heard its name, even though Salisbury with its great cathedral sits hard on the edge of the Forest in the county of Southampton.

In the old days many a farmer had bettered himself and bested the Verderers, though not many today can make Jack Newman's boast that he won *and* avoided court costs, a bill the Verderers had to pay—7,000 pounds. A farmer could risk all in such a fight, as another family had two hundred years earlier, a story we heard as if from yesterday's *Times*. The Ashby cottage had served as the inn and post office on the old London to New Forest road. Ancient law allowed a landowner to increase his holdings by digging a ditch around his property and the property he wanted to usurp—his *if* he could dig the ditch in one night without being caught. At least this is the tale we were told. Many farmers had succeeded. Mary Ashby's ancestors had failed; though they lost all their rights they were allowed to keep one acre and the stone cottage itself, located literally in the Forest. The Verderers could have taken that, as well.

Recalling these tales and trying to retell them, in the pieces that alphabets, syllables, and words are, destroys their fabric, as if I attempted to recreate a Rembrandt by inching my way along the surface, starting at the lower right corner. A piece of a piece of a nostril or fingernail—how can that convey what we ought to see whole? This is as true of pilgrimage as of painting or storytelling. Eudora Welty explains that "trips were wholes unto themselves. They were stories. Not only in form, but in their taking on direction, movement, development, change. They changed something in my life: each trip made its particular revelation, though I could not have found words for it." Sooner or later, her discovery becomes the discovery of all pilgrims, that each trip becomes a story that moves, develops, and changes us. So she and all of us who attempt to recreate the whole of stories approach them obliquely, crab-like, moving sideways rather than straight on, for otherwise they take fright and fly off. That was the only way to approach Peter Hicks, certainly; even our fellow guests, despite their citizenship, found Peter Hicks one too many for them.

We might not have heard any of his story, though, without them, for he told about Beatrice Chase and her will in their presence. But when he was asked, "How much is Higher Venton worth?" Peter Hicks started to move toward the door.

"Maybe 3,000 pound."

"More like 300,000," responded his British guest.

That finished that. Peter Hicks got a canny look in his eye and said, "Well, never mind. Got me work to do. Cattle show at Ashburton tomorrow."

We made a note to be there. Then off he went, whistling for his dogs. We soon followed, with warnings from his wife: "Dirty Weather—best stay inside today."

By then we'd learned the truth of the Dartmoor mists. They come down fast and thick, as all the old tales tell. Watching one descend, we decided to forgo the tor we had planned to climb; "You'll have another day," a local couple assured us. We had chosen this day of threatened Dirty Weather as the day. We wanted to walk Two Moors Way—not its distance, which connects Dartmoor in the south to Exmoor in the north on the sea, but just a part of it; although we wouldn't tackle mists, at least not in Dartmoor, we thought ourselves impervious to Dirty Weather, whatever that meant. Because we weren't sure and were too stubborn to ask, we stuck to our plans.

Two Moors Way, like Pilgrim's Way in Kent, appealed to us physically and spiritually. Walking is the only way to get there. Not even an off-road bike would be able to navigate the terrain of bog and moorland. Certainly no bus can reach the ancient tors, with their iron-age villages still visible, or the rings of rocks in which these original Britons practiced their religious rituals. Nor did we want to miss a climb on the burial grounds, the barrows, macabre though it sounds to eat a lunch on the long-long-since ossified bones of a people we know so little about. Although the desolate Dartmoor landscape seems so utterly appropriate for our image of iron-age Britons, they themselves would not recognize their homes, which, when they lived in them were set in and surrounded by lush forests. It was a difficult picture to superimpose on the land before and beneath us. I wondered whether they would take fright at the openness with which they would now be surrounded, almost as if stripped of all physical protection and propriety, men in their underwear.

The only alternative to feet is hoof; we saw numerous parties of riders, wise in the ways of the moors, for we never saw a lone horsewoman. But even riders had to pick their way carefully. In Exmoor, in a mist nearly as impenetrable as the one that had threatened us in Dartmoor, we continued while the two riders we met turned back, afraid of bog and broken legs. Perhaps we were foolish that day, though Exmoor is far less formidable terrain. We followed a path waymarked through pastureland; our only danger was in losing direction in the mist, but our compass kept us on course. Nevertheless each time we reached the next waymark we sighed deeply and hoped that the weather predictions for clearing skies would prevail. We were also fortunate that Exmoor farmers do not share the unsociable penchant of Cotswolds farmers to turn round or remove the signs painted or posted onto trees and fences. We could have trusted our compass and our ordnance survey map, but like most pilgrims the signs we saw were more reassuring than the map we followed. No matter how long we walk we never seem to learn that faith precedes sight.

During the days we spent in Dartmoor we saw two

iron-age villages, the one we had set out for that morning
on Two Moors Way, and one a few days earlier on the
opposite side of Widdecombe, the ancient village leaning
against a less austere terrain. As we reached it, the sun
flirted briefly with the grass-covered rocks that had
formed the huts of the villagers. We rested on rooftops
and surveyed Widdecombe below. Months and months
later when we returned to Great Britain for another bout
of pilgrim walking we sat on another high hill, this time in
the Cotswolds, overlooking another village. But what a
difference. Behind us was a golf course and beyond that a
radio tower. We experienced nothing so incongruous in
Dartmoor, unless it was the sun itself.

We had no sun on Two Moors Way; shortly after we
began walking Mrs. Hicks's Dirty Weather descended
with a violence that surprised us. We finally knew what
she meant. It is difficult to don raingear or study a map in
a downpour, and it didn't take long before we and the
map were drenched. Imagine walking rugged terrain with
a soggy raincoat clinging below mid-calf. Off and on all
day it rained; two days later I came down with a cold. I
don't think I've had one since.

But if I were searching for memories, as I had been
since high school, the remains of those ancient villages
were the places to rest, dirty weather or no. From the tor
above the village on Two Moors Way we saw the patterns
of circles, arches, and geometric forms that from within
the rocks we could not see. Stooping, stooping so low we
fell to our knees, we entered the archway of house after
house built under the sod. We've grown some since the
iron age, we told each other. Sitting in the middle of the
sacred circle, we wondered what efficacy remained within
its boundaries, what memories the rock held that would

seep into our bones. Not surprised, we noticed a ragged, rock-formed cross, a part of human Myth, as C. S. Lewis would capitalize it, that crosses all cultures.

We were fortunate as we explored the village that the dirty weather had stopped, though we met it again off Two Moors Way in an open field near a wood. It was then I realized that the rain that had come before was mere prelude to this one. Were I to paint it, the rain would need to parallel the horizon line, for it did not fall vertically but horizontally. Like everything else that day, like everything else in pilgrimage, it violated our expectations.

I think I've finally found something to remember.

Parting Ways

All beginnings are hard, but endings are even harder. Death is an ending, though it's also a beginning. Maybe all endings are like that. The end of one chapter means the beginning of the next. The end of one book leads to the beginning of another, both for writer and reader. There's no end of beginnings, only interludes along the way. And so with this chapter, which is not so much a chapter or an end but the beginning of an interlude in the journey, which will continue for each of us in another book or another pathway. It is a chance, however, to tie up loose ends before we part. I promise not to keep you.

This has been a frightening, difficult journey for me, taking me places I didn't want to go, and still don't, because each step inevitably has led me closer and closer to Death, which I think of too often as the end and not the beginning. It has forced me to face the fact that the life I know and love merely preludes something I dread more than anything in life and yet is inescapably a part of it. I don't understand this contradiction. No matter how much I think about it or how often I write about it I don't understand it. In this particular journey I waited as long as possible before confronting what was with me all along. Perhaps the death of my much-loved grandmother, which occurred as I wrote this journey, prodded me into confrontation. Would I have begun had I known that I would come face to face with my own disintegrating body? It is one thing to find myself in a desert, as we did earlier, but it is quite another to realize that the consequences of that desert could very well be death. Lost without food and water, lost without shelter from the heat or protection from the chilling night air. Lost and facing the end, when we had begun our path with such hopes. What were they? Did we hope for gold at the end of the desert? Or oil? No, we wanted what all westerners, at least in this country, want: a four-bedroom house with air-conditioning to protect us from the desert heat and an efficient furnace to warm us when we get cold.

We want nice—nice house, nice clothes, nice family, nice friends. And yet the journey, the pilgrimage, forces us to move beyond nice, because nice is not enough. In fact, nice is counterpilgrimage. If I am willing to be satisfied with nice, then my pilgrimage may never begin, or at least not move very far.

So this is what I have learned, or think I have learned. I cannot finish my pilgrimage until I confront my deepest fears of failure, of death, of sin and lust: until I face my fear of fear itself. To put it as plainly as I know how, this pilgrimage has returned me to childhood, where all my fears were giants and I accepted protection without question from the adults in my life. As an adult, I loathe admitting a need that was a natural part of my early vocabulary, for big girls don't cry.

I had two fearful dreams when I was young. In one the moon, as it shone on the Atlantic coast of Connecticut, got so bright that it shattered into millions of glass-like slivers and stabbed fish and swans—and me, straight in the eyes. In the other, the bridge my parents rode broke into two pieces and they drove off the edge into the water below. I awoke from the first dream screaming in terror to find my mother and father standing over my bed. In the other I awoke to my own sobbing voice, and no one was near. These dreams represent my terrors, terrors we all have in one form or another. There are simply too many folk tales and nursery rhymes to deny how fundamentally death terrorizes us—and so often these folk tales and nursery rhymes take place on the road. They become the giants and windmills that block our path and threaten to halt our pilgrimage. Until we do grave and terrible battle with them we cannot continue.

It's hard, however, to confront the Dark Knight on the road, in the words of one old ballad, when we are alone. We're lost and wandering children, and yet somehow, miraculously, we find each other and we find the path, even when we think we're nowhere near it. And then, if we later *must* face our fears alone, we have been strengthened for the contest by the tales and companionship we have experienced. We can recall visions of giant, blooming azalea bushes that rested us in the Doone Valley or laugh when we remember how we mistook a cow for a bull or searched and searched for a footpath only to discover we had been paralleling it all along.

Perhaps we took to the path somehow knowing that we would get lost, but that we would also get found. We knew that John Wayne or Piers Plowman or John Milton or even Edmund Spenser would come along and set us right, if we were wise enough to heed their instructions. If we had listened to the Duke, we might not now be facing this dangling, untied narrative thread, you and I in the desert, clutching our guidebook and our parkas. We've traveled to Germany, to Britain, and beyond, back in time to pilgrims on their way to the Holy Land, and forward when pilgrims can hop an El Al flight and be singing the Israeli national anthem in a few hours. All from the hollowed-out place in the sand by our rock in the desert. We've dreamed and argued and debated the merits of tourism, as well as the puzzling directions of our pilgrim guidebook.

The desert has its beauties—vast, undulating stretches of space interrupted by lush gardens—as well as its terrors and problems. An emblem of life, where the contours of sand, with its moving blend of whites and tans, create a rhythm and fill the seemingly empty space with heartbeat and potential. I've wanted to leave the desert; I've been planning, somehow, for a way out, but I find that I cannot knot this thread, anymore than I can keep Death out of this interlude.

It is nearly fall, a season that doesn't mean much in the desert but one that outside the desert awaits me. It closes in on Death, or Death closes in on summer. But before that comes a burst of life, as if nature intended to make the most of itself—to show Death what it is up against. It is not the time to go on pilgrimage; it is the time to return to the routines, but now knowing that pilgrimage exists *within* the routines and deserts, and not in spite of them.

I know this because of a church we visited, although I can't remember where my husband found it. On the outside it appeared to be merely another old, decaying building, with the graveyard overgrown with nettles and Queen Anne's Lace. We could see deep cracks in the walls and smell the spores of must in the air. Yet when we walked in, the marble floors were worn down in a reassuring path that led from narthex to altar. The mahogany pews might have been scratched but nevertheless they glowed with love and elbow grease. The cracked leather kneelers showed that people here still bowed to pray, regardless of stiff knee joints and arthritic fingers. Because the day was unusually warm, the dank air was as refreshing as a desert spring.

This wasn't a large church, nor was it as small as others we had visited, such as the one in Exmoor caught in a crook of rock and reachable only on foot. As we struggled our way up the steep path to its door, I thought of the arguments about parking facilities and easy access so many churches in our communities have; getting to church shouldn't prove taxing. This postage stamp building made me wonder which view was closer to correct. Obviously too small to support its own vicar, the church shared its priest with other small country churches, and the wardens had posted service times outside the door. I was glad to read that the church still saw the enactment of worship within its doors.

But the day we found oasis inside this other church somewhere in Great Britain I wasn't thinking about size. I wasn't even thinking about the worn floors or the polished pews; only now do I recall them. My attention, rather, was focused on the unusually open narthex, which was not walled off from the sanctuary itself but formed one large room. In the far end of the church, the far end of the narthex, stood the strangest collection of tools— carpenter's tools, a sawhorse, a bellows, an old plow, the kind an ox might pull. They stood there as if there were no distinction to be made between the world of work and the world of worship, between the world of the desert and the world of the pilgrim. In that church the two became part of each other to share an exchange of energy that served each other, so that worship became ordinary and work extraordinary—and pilgrimage between the two worlds eased.

I had encountered no clearer sign posts than these old tools housed in a church. They showed me the whole of the path, finally, in this small and seemingly insignificant part. Here was a church that lived within its Liberties. And it told me where I and all pilgrims belong, so that no matter how reluctant we still long to go.

Rich man, poor man, bag lady, thief—here is our tale.

—September 1991

The text of Notes of a Reluctant Pilgrim is set in
10/14 Palatino. Designed by Hermann Zapf in 1948,
Palatino is a rich reinterpretation of Oldstyle type
and has a subtly calligraphic feel. The type was set
on a Linotron 202/N by the Photocomposition Department
of Zondervan Publishing House; Sue Koppenol, compositor.
The interior typography design is by Louise Bauer.
The cover design and photograph are by Mark Veldheer.
Printed by Malloy Lithographers of Ann Arbor, Michigan.